I would like to thank you for this well-thought out and innovative programme which deals with the Physical, Emotional, Mental and Spiritual Health of the individual. I enjoyed the total package. On a daily basis I am utilizing all that I have been taught to encourage others to participate in this life changing experience. May God continue to bless you!

Cassey Sandiford, - Insurance Employee, Barbados

I first learned about the Emotional Health Restoration Programme through an advertisement on the radio. I was immediately of the view that it was a programme which would benefit me and I ascertained further details. This programme was indeed life-changing; I gained a wealth of knowledge and have been able to apply and reinforce many lifestyle practices which improved my emotional well-being. Pastor Marshall did an excellent job presenting the course material and providing Godly counsel. I have no regrets registering for this programme and would encourage others to do the same.

Shari Murrell, Trainee Accountant, Barbados

Having endured a very traumatic time in my life I received the information leaflet for the above programme "at just the right time" via a multimedia avenue. There are no words to fully describe how this programme has helped me tremendously; the introductory paragraph on the front page says:

"A twelve – part series which provides an avenue for the restoration of emotional, psychological and spiritual health by engaging in psychological processes, journeys and steps to experience balance, emotional freedom and harmony in your life"

This programme has done for me what it "says on the can" so to speak. It has taken me to a new level and ensured that I travelled my journey restoring my emotional, psychological and spiritual health, I have experienced balance, emotional freedom and harmony in my life; it has given me the tools to be able think about, reframe events and journey on in a more productive and stable manner. I found all aspects of the programme engaging doing the fast as a group was very encouraging and this helped me to look at and consider my diet in a little more detail.

Having the option of undertaking this programme via zoom was an opportunity not to be missed; Pastor Marshall ensured that I received all the required resources in a timely way, and having the resources guaranteed that this programme is always at hand and can be re-visited if needs be. The programme is structured in such a way that it ensures you take into account and address your wellbeing in a holistic way. A great reminder of the spiritual aspects of your life that help to bring back to memory Bible verses that may be buried deep in your memory given the trauma that you may have gone through. There is nothing intrusive about this programme, and it a great opportunity to explore the areas of your life that you feel need a good over haul; an excellent programme for everyone that reaches across generations, culture and spirituality / faith. I feel grateful that I have been able to undertake this programme.

Without a shadow of a doubt I would recommend this programme to everyone. It certainly needs to sit with all the recognised programmes of well-known clinicians etc. Out of ten I would give this programme a twelve. Thank you Pastor Marshall for following God's leading, having the tenacity, resolve and the fore sight for knowing that such a programme is required. God bless you as you take on the task of developing more programmes.

Coral Millin, Social Worker, United Kingdom

Pastoral 7
Perspectives & Issues

Emotional Health
Restoration
Programme

Victor Marshall

MSc (Health Psych), MA (Pract Th), MA (Past Th), M Ed (Ed Psych & Sped Ed)

A twelve - part series which provides an avenue for the restoration of emotional, psychological and spiritual health by engaging in psychological processes, journeys and steps to experience balance, freedom and harmony in your life.

author HOUSE

AuthorHouse™ UK
1663 Liberty Drive
Bloomington, IN 47403 USA
www.authorhouse.co.uk
Phone: UK TFN: 0800 0148641 (Toll Free inside the UK)
*   UK Local: (02) 0369 56322 (+44 20 3695 6322 from outside the UK)*

Published by AuthorHouse 09/14/2023

ISBN: 979-8-8230-8409-3 (sc)

Library of Congress Control Number: 2023914597

Print information available on the last page.

Any people depicted in stock imagery provided by Getty Images are models, and such images are being used for illustrative purposes only.
Certain stock imagery © Getty Images.

Unless otherwise noted, all Scripture references are from the New King James Version.

Texts credited to NKJV are taken from the New King James Version. Copyright © 1982 by Thomas Nelson, Inc. Used by permission. All rights reserved.

Scripture quotations marked (NIV) are taken from the Holy Bible, New International Version®, NIV®. Copyright © 1973, 1978, 1984, 2011 by Biblica, Inc.™ Used by permission of Zondervan. All rights reserved worldwide. www.zondervan.com. The "NIV" and "New International Version" are trademarks registered in the United States Patent and Trademark Office by Biblica, Inc.™

Scripture quotations taken from the Amplified® Bible (AMP), Copyright © 2015 by The Lockman Foundation. Used by permission. lockman.org"

Scripture quotations marked NLT are taken from the Holy Bible, New Living Translation, copyright 1996, 2004. Used by permission of Tyndale House Publishers, Inc., Wheaton, Illinois 60189. All rights reserved.

Scriptures marked KJV are taken from the KING JAMES VERSION (KJV): KING JAMES VERSION, public domain.

Acknowledgements:
Thanks to the members of the various teams for being willing to work with me for this programme.

Caution: *This book and the DVDs/PowerPoint series do not establish a doctor-patient or counsellor-client relationship with the reader/participant. Persons who are on medication or who presently are engaged in counselling/ therapeutic sessions and who wish to change their lifestyle significantly should do so under the direction of a medical physician or counselling practitioner who is familiar with the effects of a change in an emotional healthy lifestyle.*

The author assumes full responsibility for the accuracy of all facts and quotations as cited in this book.

This book is printed on acid-free paper.

Because of the dynamic nature of the Internet, any web addresses or links contained in this book may have changed since publication and may no longer be valid. The views expressed in this work are solely those of the author and do not necessarily reflect the views of the publisher, and the publisher hereby disclaims any responsibility for them.

Other Books by Victor D. Marshall

A Journey of the Bold and the Young: Living on the Edge

Raising the Wounded: Grasping for Hope in the Midst of Despair

Set the Captives Free: Experiencing Healing Through Holistic Restoration

Set the Captives Free: 12 Studies for Groups or Individuals

On the Road to Forgiveness: Experiencing Healing on the Way

Dedication

The first enthusiastic cohort of participants in 2014 who attended in person at the Millennium Centre in Sheffield, United Kingdom . Additionally, I am dedicating this volume to the spirited and dedicated group in Handsworth, Birmingham who followed the programme in 2015. This book is also dedicated to the determined and enduring groups in Barbados, who participated in first three programmes. Additionally, the advice, encouragement and support from Priscilla Prevost, denominational Health Director in the Eastern Caribbean have assisted me greatly in getting this programme into the public arena.

Contents

Acknowledgements xi

Welcome to the Emotional Health Restoration Programme! xiii

About This Book xv

Suggested Reading List xvii

Introduction xxi

1. Identifying Emotional Instability and Contributory Factors 1

2. Gauging Your Degree of Emotional Wounded-ness 25

3. Lifestyle Interventions for Emotional Ill-health 47

4. Foods to Boost Your Mood 65

5. Forgiveness: Its Healing Power (Part 1) 85

6. Forgiveness: Its Healing Power (Part I1) 107

7. A Journey to the Underworld 129

8. Coping Strategies for Emotional Ill-health 153

9. Improving Your Quality of Life for Emotional Health 173

10. Rising Beyond Childhood Adversity 193

11. Fulfilling Psychological Needs Enhances Emotional Health 217

12. How to Improve Brain Function 241

APPENDIX

Appendix A: Emotional Healthy Lifestyle Scorecard (Alternative) 265

Appendix B: Resource for the De-cluttering Task 271

Appendix C: Spiritual Resources 277

Appendix D: Self-awareness Perspectives 283

References 289

Acknowledgements

Sincere thanks are due to the many individuals who directly or indirectly assisted me in ensuring that the *Emotional Health Restoration* Programme was ready to be conducted. I give thanks to the Almighty Healing Creator for every bit of Divine inspiration which I receive to get this programme into the public arena.

I am indebted to the President of the East Caribbean Conference of Seventh-day Adventists, Pastor Anthony S. Hall, who entrusted the Family and Men's Ministries Departments into my hands to minister to constituents, provide Godly counsel and to develop resources for the field. Thank you Sir!

To the various members in the Seventh-day Adventist Churches in Sheffield, United Kingdom, who heard about the programme and wanted to be a participant, I say a heartfelt thank you.

The Boards and members of the St James and City Central Districts of Seventh-day Adventist Churches in Barbados, who assisted me in bringing this programme to the districts, by distributing the e-flyer, recommending the programme by word-of-mouth or supported a participant in joining the programme, I am grateful for your efforts.

I appreciate the encouragement and support from individuals such as Allison Blackwood, Beverley Price, Denise Reid and Patricia Smith who were participants in my first train-the-trainer course in 2020.

Last, but by no means least, I say a special thank you to Marcia Webster who constantly checked on the progress of the programme during the editing stage. Her constant questions concerning the project and reminders about my deadline with the publishers were medicine for the writer's block which I had experienced temporarily.

Welcome to the Emotional Health Restoration Programme!

CONGRATULATIONS on choosing to attend the most comprehensive programme available on the subject of emotional and spiritual restoration. It is pleasing to know that you are interested in restoring a particular type of relationship by focusing on your emotional, physical, psychological, social and spiritual wellbeing. This programme has helped hundreds of individuals since it was introduced in 2011.

Whether you, a loved one or a close friend is struggling with emotional wounded-ness, it is heartening to know that you have decided to attend this programme which seeks to help such individuals and also act as a resource for those who desire to take the journey towards total wholeness. Furthermore, this programme is appropriate for individuals who simply want to improve their emotional, physical, psychological, social or spiritual wellbeing and follow an emotionally healthy lifestyle. In order to participate, you need to have a desire to face whatever unresolved painful issue(s) you have, be committed for the entire series and be determined not to live in the past where there is negativity and emotional pain.

Local facilitators should remember that the programme is an educational resource, based on pastoral care perspectives, therapeutic awareness and is aimed at aiding individuals in experiencing emotional, physical, psychological, social and spiritual restoration. This is not a substitute for counselling, psychotherapy or any other formal therapeutic programme which can be had from a trained counsellor or therapist.

The books, POWERPOINTS and DVDs and /or volunteer staff do not at any time establish a doctor-patient or counsellor-client relationship. People who are attending therapeutic sessions should continue to work with their professional helper.

About This Book

The *Emotional Health Restoration Programme* is an aid to your progress in improving, restoring and maintaining your emotional, psychological, social, and spiritual health and well-being. This workbook has been designed to include all the significant elements that would be involved in a live presentation of the programme if you were watching a DVD.

The important sections of the programme include:

> **Insightful Perspective:** This is designed to prepare you for the material included in the presentations (as well as to consolidate the suggestions made in the programme). As you read the suggested chapters, it will afford you the opportunity to have a knowledge of the concepts and ideas presented in each session. This will assist you in benefiting more from the presentations.

> **The Slides** have been provided so that you can move along with the presenter more closely and also take notes.

> **Emotional Healthy Lifestyle Matters** bring out the lessons from the presentations in practical ways which can be included in your personal daily life, with ease and enjoyment.

Suggested Reading List

The following are the **required** books for participants who plan to follow the programme:

- *Set the Captives Free (Resource Guide): Experiencing Healing through Holistic Restoration* by Victor D Marshall

- *Raising the Wounded: Grasping for Hope in the Midst of Despair* by John D. Doughlin

- *Set the Captives Free: Twelve Studies for Groups or Individuals* by Victor D. Marshall

- *On the Road to Forgiveness: Experiencing Healing on the Way* by Victor D. Marshall

- *Emotional Health Restored* by Victor D. Marshall

The following are the **recommended** books for participants who plan to follow the programme:

- *Forgive to Live* by Dick Tibbits, Ph D

- *Ministry of Healing* by Ellen G. white

- *Mind, Character & Personality, Volumes 1 & 2* by Ellen G. white

- *Counsels on Health* by Ellen G. White

- *Medical Ministry* by Ellen G. White

- *Counsels on Diet and Foods* by Ellen G. White

- *Temperance* by Ellen G. White

- *Welfare Ministry* by Ellen G. White

'Set the Captives Free'

Emotional Health *Restoration* Programme

Offers

A Week-end Residential Emotional Health & Prayer Conference

An Opportunity for you to take the journey towards total wholeness

You will enjoy three (3) days away from the everyday pressures in a relaxed environment. Additionally, there are trained personnel providing life-transforming presentations, coupled with daily spiritual practices.

The Programme includes

❖ Participation in a three-day diet detox

❖ Creation and interpretation of your genogram

❖ Daily interactive presentations

❖ Indepth small group study

❖ Instructions on food choices, its benefits and preparation

❖ Listening sessions with trained counsellors

❖ Presentations addressing issues relating to dysfunctional behaviour

For further information, contact:

Mobile :

Email:

In order to gain the most out of this programme, it is recommended that you set aside two hours, one day per week – preferably the same day each week - for the next twelve (12) weeks. For example, you can opt to host the programme on Monday evenings (6:00 p.m- 8:00 p.m) OR Tuesday mid-day (12 noon – 2 p.m).

Facilitators can split the two hours, where the presentation/teaching is done for 75 minutes and the small group session for 30 mins. Alternatively, another day can be selected for the small group session when you can use an hour for this session.

*I*ntroduction

"Is there no balm in Gilead? Is there no physician there? Why then has not the [spiritual] health of the daughter of my people been restored?[1] This biblical perspective alerts us of the need for healing and restoration in our life. Importantly, we are reminded that "the brain is the organ and instrument of the mind, and controls the whole body. In order for the other parts of the system to be healthy, the brain must be healthy. And in order for the brain to be healthy, the blood must be pure. If by correct habits of eating and drinking the blood is kept pure, the brain will be properly nourished."[2] It is against this perspective that this programme, which focuses on comprehensive health and wellbeing, has been designed.

The above counsel demands that we take time out to look after ourselves on various levels, be it emotional, physical, psychological or social. It is the Heavenly Creator's desire that every human being be whole and be restored to Him, hence the reason Christ, the Healing Redeemer came into the world so that we can experience life abundantly.[3] With this in mind, we seek to ensure that one's emotional health and spiritual maturity are well developed, hence the reason for this **Emotional Health** *Restoration* **Programme.**

As a community of people, it is important that we see the need to assist others who may be in need of holistic restoration. However, this can be achieved by recommending appropriate programmes and resources that would benefit these individuals. Additionally, our emotional and spiritual maturity are critical aspects of our personhood which can be developed through avenues such as counselling, intercessory prayer and therapy.

Furthermore, everyone needs to be aware of his/her total wellbeing which can be achieved by using tools and engaging in suitable programmes. In this programme, participants will learn about how to bring about emotional balance in their relationships, be it with friends, neighbours, relatives or spouses. Additionally, you will examine different aspects of forgiveness and examine how to address dysfunctional relational patterns. Moreover, you will create, analyse and interpret your own genogram which can help you depict an inter-generational family map about your emotional, medical and social history.

Apart from the theoretical aspects, you will be assessed using tools and instruments weekly to examine areas such as your emotional health and spiritual maturity and emotional type/styles of relating. Other areas which you are assessed on is your degree of emotional wounded-ness and the impact of past painful issues on your emotional wellbeing. As you begin this programme, may you experience a powerful journey and acquire the help that you desire!

Self-Evaluations

Please complete the **Inventory of Emotional Wounded-ness** (I-EW) before proceeding further with the programme. You will be instructed when to take the assessment. This is the 'before' self-evaluation which gauges your level of emotional wounded-ness/hurt at the beginning of the programme. If your level of wounded-ness is worse than you believe it should be, you should not be ashamed, feel guilty or feel insecure. By seeking to improve *your emotional health*, you can be aided in experiencing a measure of improvement, thereby, developing positive emotional health further.

Inventory of Emotional Wounded-ness/Emotional Hurt - 'Before'

The inventory below allows you to gauge the level of your emotional and spiritual maturity to determine what emotional stage you are at on the human life cycle of development. Instructions will be given as to how to conduct the assessment.

Category of Emotional Wounded-ness	Scores				
	0 – 10	11– 20	21 – 30	30 - 39	40 – 48
	Intensity of the Effect of Emotional Wounded-ness				
	Least Affected	Mildly Affected	Moderately Affected	Severely Affected	Profoundly Affected
Level 1 (Whole)					
Level 2 (Bruised)					
Level 3 (Wounded)					
Level 4 (Broken)					
Level 5 (Damaged)					

EXAMPLE: 0   +   3   + 4   +   6   +   4   =   17

                (0 x 2)   +   (1x3) +   (2x2)   +   (3x2)   +   (4x1) =

This score of 17 falls in the second intensity level of being mildly affected in the chart above.

SOURCE: Taken from Victor D. Marshall, *On the Road to Forgiveness Experiencing Healing On the Way* (Bloomington, IN: Authorhouse, June 2015), pp. 247. See Appendix C for the original version. However, the revised version is located in *Set the Captives Free* **Emotional Health Restoration Programme** Tool Kit.

MENTAL HEALTH CHECKLIST

Item No.	1-Not True 2-Sometimes True 3- True Most Times 4-Very True 5-Definitely True					
	Items	1	2	3	4	5
1.	**Emotional Well-being** Usually, I have been cheerful compared to most of my peers/friends/colleagues	1	2	3	4	5
2.	Although I have been struggling with various life issues, I have managed to remain calm, peaceful and in good spirits.	1	2	3	4	5
3.	I am not generally very happy and nor do I enjoy life.	1	2	3	4	5
4.	Generally, I am interested in societal issues, international situations and life matters.	1	2	3	4	5
5.	I am usually full of life and motivated.	1	2	3	4	5
6.	My main areas of my life such as church, family, health and work are dis-satisfying.	1	2	3	4	5
Sub-Total (Add the numbers you circled in each box)						
	Psychological Wellbeing					
7.	I am comfortable with and have accepted my limitations (e.g: disability), as well as my strengths (e.g: piano playing)	1	2	3	4	5
8.	I like most aspects of my personality.	1	2	3	4	5
9.	The view which I have of myself is negative because of my difficulties, both physical and spiritual.	1	2	3	4	5
10.	I have been slothful in engaging in personal development such as attending health seminars or family life conferences.	1	2	3	4	5
11.	I have a feeling of continued development and therefore, think that I am growing.	1	2	3	4	5
12.	When I think about it, I have not really improved a lot over the years.	1	2	3	4	5
13.	I am unaware of my real potentials, gifts and the resources which I have that can be useful for the benefit of other.	1	2	3	4	5
14.	I have confidence in my own opinions, even if they are different from the way most other people think.	1	2	3	4	5
15.	I tend to be influenced by people with strong opinions.	1	2	3	4	5
16.	I am quite good at managing the many responsibilities of my daily life.	1	2	3	4	5
17.	The demands of everyday life often get me down.	1	2	3	4	5
18.	I have a sense of direction and purpose in life.	1	2	3	4	5
19.	"I don't have a good sense of what it is I'm trying to accomplish in life.	1	2	3	4	5

VICTOR MARSHALL

Interpretation of Ratings/Scores

Ratings/Values

Languishing Mental Health.

0 – 50   Generally, a very low level of overall mental health, to the point that it is unsatisfactory.

51 – 100   The score in this range reflects a sense of being partially mentally healthy.

Moderately Mentally Healthy

101 – 150   A moderate sense of mental health and suggests that you are at the intermediate level of well-being

Flourishing Mental Health

151 – 200   The score indicates that individuals are flourishing reasonably well based on the high level of mental health and they are living a satisfactory and fulfilling life.

201 - 250   Generally, this range of scores indicates a positive and very high mental health and that individuals are flourishing very well.

NB: See the full version in *Set the Captives Free* **Emotional Health Restoration Programme** Tool Kit.

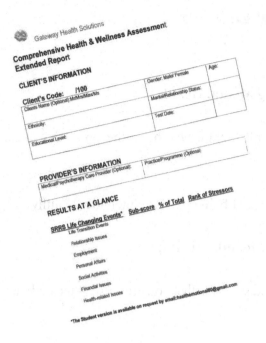

The resources here can aid anyone in measuring:

- Degree of Emotional wounded-ness

- Style of relating

- Level of Mental Health

- Stress load and its level

The Comprehensive Health & Wellness Assessment can help you:

- Track your growth at various intervals of the programme

- Identify your degree of emotional wounded-ness and recommendations

- Determine whether you are flourishing or languishing

This assessment has been created after hours of research and practical experience in working with numerous participants. It is also available in an electronic format, but must be returned via email (healthemotional80@gmail.com) for scoring in about two weeks.

Comprehensive Health Care Plan (PARTICIPANT'S COPY)

PARTICIPANT'S ASSESSMENT			
SECTION 1: PERSONAL DATA		**DATE:** / /20	
Participant's Name: Ms/Miss/Mr/Mrs		Age Range: 15-20 ( ) 21-25 ( ) 26-30 ( ) 31-35 ( ) 36-40 ( ) 41-45( ) 46 -50() 51-55 ( ) 56-60 ( ) 61-65( ) 66-70 ( ) 70 + ( )	
Emergency Contact Details: Tel. No: Cell No: Email: Relationship to You:		Other Care Plan [e.g: Medical care/medication counselling/psychologist/psychotherapy] YES: ( ) NO ( )	
SECTION 2: HEALTH INDICATORS Health data over the past 12 months prior to engaging in the programme			
STRESS LOAD	**ANXIETY LEVEL**	**BODY MASS INDEX**	**BLOOD PRESSURE**
Stress Load: __ Stress Level: __ **Member status (Please check one)** ☐ A. Stress load < 200 ☐ B. Stress level < 25 ☐ C. Committed to Following the Intervention activities ☐ D. Is not willing to change behaviour /following the intervention programme	Performance: _ Social Interaction: _ **Member status (Please check one)** ☐ A. Performance Score < 49 ☐ B. Social Interaction < 49 ☐ C. Committed to Following the Intervention activities ☐ D. Is not willing to change behaviour /following the intervention programme	BMI:_____ kg/m² **Member status (Please check one)** ☐ A. BMI < 25 kg/m² ☐ B. 25 < BMI < 30 (unless pregnant) ☐ C. BMI > 30 kg/m² ☐ D. Committed to Following the Intervention activities ☐ E. Is not willing to change behaviour /following the intervention programme	☐ **Newly Diagnosed hypertension** BP:_____ mm/Hg **Member status (Please check one)** ☐ A. Blood Pressure < 120/80 mm/Hg ☐ B. Blood Pressure > 120/80 mm/Hg ☐ C. Committed to Following the Intervention activities ☐ **D.** Is not willing to change behaviour /following the intervention programme
PRESENTING ISSUE(S) What are the participant's current health situation (physical, emotional)?			
PARTICIPANT'S BRIEF HISTORY Participant's relevant family, physical/biological, psychological and social history			
ANY OTHER RELEVANT INFORMATION			
RISKS AND CO-MORBIDITIES Note any associated risks and co-morbidities.			
DEPRESSION SCORE/ RATING			
Referral Programme in relation to health indicators: (e.g: two types of physical exercise at least 4 times per week; increase of water intake; weight management; sleep detox; healthy eating)			

NB: After the assessment results are returned, a Comprehensive Health Care Plan, with recommendations, can be put in place to assist you in addressing the pronounced health issues.

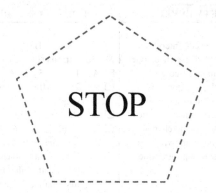

STOP

Have you taken the Comprehensive Health and Wellness Assessment? It is strongly recommended that you do so before continuing. Ask your facilitator for details.

Session One

Identifying Emotional Instability and Contributory Factors

DURING this session, pay attention to:

1) How emotional disturbance occurs and the consequences.

2) Emotional dissonance and its impact on emotional wellbeing.

3) The Emotionally-stuck syndrome and self-awareness

You will notice in this *Companion Folder* that you have the outline of the PowerPoint presentation for **Session One**, so that you may follow along.

To complete this programme successfully, you will need:

- *Set the Captives Free: 12 Studies for Groups or Individuals* by Victor D. Marshall

- *Raising the Wounded: Grasping for Hope in the Midst of Despair* by John D. Doughlin

- *Set the Captives Free: Experiencing Healing Through Holistic Restoration* by Victor D. Marshall

- *On the Road to Forgiveness: Experiencing Healing on the Way* by Victor D. Marshall

- The *Emotional Health Restoration Companion* Folder

Interactive Learning Approaches

There are various ways to interact with this material. One way is to take notes while you listen/ watch the presentation. This can also include filling in the blank spaces in the workbook and the companion folder. Some individuals prefer the visual slides, while others prefer to hear the presentation from the Programme Presenter. Whatever approach is most beneficial for you is what you should use as you take this journey towards restoring your health on various levels (e.g: emotional, psychological, social). Feel free to complete the answers at your pace and wherever you feel most comfortable.

Session One

Identifying Emotional Instability and Contributory Factors

During the PowerPoint presentations, feel free to follow along with the slides that correspond with those in the session. You can fill in the blank spaces with the missing words. Use the blanks in the margin with the letters that match to the letters on the blanks in the PowerPoint slides. (For example, for blank [a], write the answer on the line next to the section of the slide marked [a].

1.

> ## EMOTIONAL HEALTH RESTORATION PROGRAMME
>
> Identifying Emotional Dys-functionality
> and Possible Solutions

2.

> ## Session 1
>
> Identifying Emotional Instability
> and Contributory Factors

Being Stuck Emotionally is Prevalent

Every time we experience a severe emotional _____a_____ which has been unresolved, we become _____b____ and at times we are unaware of it.

Emotionally Stuck – What is it?

Individuals who are emotionally stuck means that _____c_____ we know what are our goals and desires, but _____d_____ we do not feel confident or equipped to accomplish these personal achievements.

Emotionally Stuck – What is it?

Inwardly, there is no _____ e_____, which means that we are not having new experiences, we are unable to progress and we are no further than we were previously at the emotional, psychological or spiritual level.

3.

a. _____

b. _____

4.

c. _____

d. _____

5.

e. _____

Emotionally Stuck Syndrome

Such individuals become caught in the pursuit-withdrawal and _____**f**_____ cycles. This negative emotional state gnaws at your emotional well-being and eventually creates distress which leads to emotional _____**g**_____

(Gottman, J., *What Predicts Divorce? The Relationship Between Marital Processes and Marital Outcomes* (Hillsdale, NJ: Erlbaum, 1994).

6.

f. _____

g. _____

Emotionally Stuck Syndrome

These negative emotional experiences are provoked by holding unhealthy ____**h**_____ beliefs about an adverse event. When we engage in this type of thinking, we are emotionally stuck. This type of thinking pattern is a key feature of emotional _____**i**_____.

Avy Joseph, Maggie Chapman, *Visual CBT: Using Pictures to Help You Apply Cognitive Behaviour Therapy to Change Your Life* (NJ: John Wiley & Sons, 2012); Catana Brown & Virginia C. Stoffiel, *Occupational Therapy in Mental Health: A Vision for Participation* (PA: F. A Davis, 2010), p. 269.

7.

h. _____

i. _____

Emotionally Stuck Syndrome

8.

Consequences of Emotional Disturbance

Emotional disturbance in our thinking and opinions results in social consequences such as ___j___, boredom, limited association, ___k___ negative conversation and lack of knowledge. Emerging out of this is a situation where we ignore new ideas, the changing conditions around us and hence, continue to live in denial.

9.

j. _____

k. _____

Consequences of Emotional Disturbance

The longer we take to resolve the issue, the greater the possibility of bringing about an emotional ___l___ in our life. When there is a great distance between the unresolved painful experience and the present time, it is an indication that there are ___m___ disorders.

10.

l. _____

m. _____

An Emotionally Imbalanced Relationship

Unresolved
Painful issues

Your life &
relationships

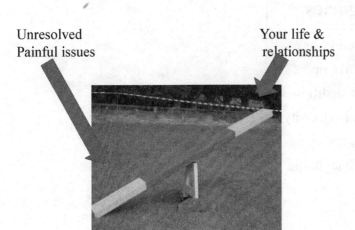

11.

Issues which can create an imbalance in our relationship are:

_____

_____

_____

_____

_____

_____

Fig. 8.1: Hierarchy of Holistic Restoration Model

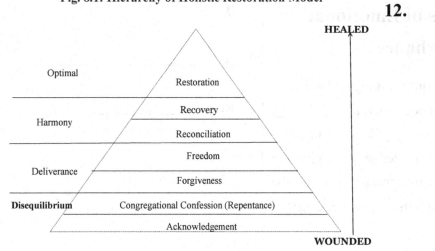

12.

13.

Hierarchy of Holistic Restoration Model

The starting point for addressing emotional disturbance is to recognise two (2) _____**n**_____ at the bottom/ base of the pyramid: acknowledgement and confession/repentance must be addressed adequately before we can ___**o**___ upward to the next rung on the pyramid.

n. _____

o. _____

14.

The Twelve 'Risk' Categories

1. **Emotional Instability**
2. Emotional Hurt
3. Lifestyle
4. Nutrition
5. Forgiveness
6. Abuse
7. Unresolved Issues
8. Inability to Cope
9. Medical Condition
10. Childhood Adversity
11. Psychological Needs
12. Mental Functioning

1. Emotional Instability Risk

Individuals who desire to _____p_____ emotionally, would need to acknowledge that there are unresolved problems. Other words for acknowledgement are: ____q____, recognise or agree.

15.

p. _____

q. _____

1. Emotional Instability Risk

A key component to this programme is helping individuals ____r____ emotional, ____s____, and spiritual equilibrium to their well-being by establishing and ___t___ a predictable routine.

16.

r. _____

s. _____

t. _____

Helpful Counsel

Margaret Swarbrick, in her article on wellness, suggests the need for a 'self-defined daily routine' since 'it can help offset inner chaos and provide a pattern that helps a person regain control and order in his/her life'.

Swarbrick, M. (2006). 'A Wellness Approach' in *Psychiatric Rehabilitation Journal* 29 (4), pp.311-314 (312).

17.

Self-awareness

One way by which to gauge our emotional balance is by developing our self-awareness. It is the ability to understand the way a person has a particular ___u_____ and why she behaves in a particular way. This ability is essential for improving relationships and adjusting one's ____v_____ in order to interact with others positively. Self-awareness helps emotionally-distraught individuals to ____w____ and manage their self-control.

18.

u. _____

v. _____

w. _____

Definition of Self Image

It refers to the _____x_____ picture a person has of him/herself and her qualities. These ideas are also about how individuals hold the conception or ____y_____ they have of themselves.

19.

x. _____

y. _____

Function of Self-image

A person's self-image is his/her individual ___z_____. Since a person has many identities linked to the many roles in life, it defines the role in our relationships.

Orv Nease, *Feeling Fooled: How to Stop Letting Your Negative Emotions Wreck Your Life (Vienna, VA:* Xulon Press, 2001), p. 109.

20.

z. _____

Reasons for Developing Self-awareness

Our self-awareness impacts on our self-image. It is important to develop self-awareness in order to alter one's _____**a2**_____, thereby, changing our emotions. Self-awareness enables individuals to recognise how they control their behaviour, emotions and personality and therefore, make appropriate changes.

Ways to Develop Your Self-image

Our self-image along with self-awareness are the predecessors to self-esteem. Individuals with high/positive self-image, _____**b2**_____themselves in a manner in which they desire their friends, peers and associates to perceive them.

Errol A. Gibbs and Philip A. Grey, *Five Foundations of Human Development* (IN: AuthorHouse, 2011), p.315.

21.

a2._____

22.

b2._____

23.

Who AM I?

Self-Image

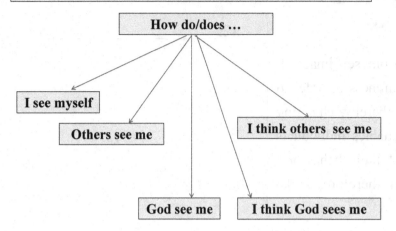

24.

How do/does ...

- I see myself
- Others see me
- I think others see me
- God see me
- I think God sees me

25.

Divine Assurance I:

Know that the Lord, He *is* God;
It is He *who* has made us, and [b]not we ourselves;
We are His people and the sheep of His pasture.

Psalm 100: 3

26.

Divine Assurance II:

It is essential that we focus on the major factor which determines our identity. The Divine assurance indicates that "we are His workmanship, created in Christ Jesus for good works, which God prepared beforehand that we should walk in them."

Ephesians 2: 10

Summary

❖ Unresolved painful emotional, psychological and spiritual issues lead to emotional disturbance (being emotionally stuck).

❖ Our unresolved negative emotional experiences impact on relationships and contribute to difficulties with our emotional health.

❖ Unhealthy beliefs, opinions and thoughts bring about consequences such as social isolation and a rejection of new ideas.

❖ Leaving an emotional difficulty unresolved for a prolonged period of time could bring about a psychological disorder such as depression.

> **a)** Read 'A Biblical Perspective of Restoration' on **pages 6-7** in *Set the Captives Free (Resource Guide/Manual).*
>
> **b)** Remember to read Chapter 1 –Open Wounds Hurt in *Raising the Wounded: Grasping for Hope in the Midst of Despair.*

Insightful Perspectives

Emotional Healthy Lifestyle Matters

Let us turn to the *emotional healthy lifestyle matters* section. These are activities and tasks we can engage in to aid our emotional, physical, psychological, relational, social and spiritual development. Some of these can be done on your own at home. For this programme, all the emotional healthy lifestyle matters are based on the **HEALINGS** health principles. The acronym stands for:

> H – Hope
> E – Environment
> A – Activities (Exercise)
> L – Lying Down (Rest)
> I - Interpersonal Relationships
> N - Nutrition
> G - Guidance (Spiritual)
> S - Sunlight

1. 'Flush' the mind with wholesome activities.

'Flushing' the mind refers to the sudden rush of intense uplifting activities or the imposing of large quantities of wholesome material into the mind to clear it of the toxins built up from the negative emotions, feelings and moods such as anger, bitterness, fear and sadness. This activity relates to both your internal and external **Environment** (World), the second component of the HEALINGS health principles. This means that you, the individual, must take the first step in improving your health by creating a positive internal and external environment as much as possible.

Dr. Nedergaard from the National Institute of Neurological Disorders and Stroke (NINDS) which is associated with the National Institutes of Health in the USA (2013 Research) found that adequate sleep cleansed the brain/mind of the toxins built up during the day and even over a longer period of time. A lack of an opportunity to clear the waste (toxin) in the brain, leads to a build-up of amyloid protein, a toxin which poisons/kills organs and body cells. Furthermore, an accumulation/build-up of this toxin is linked to degenerative diseases such as Alzheimer's disease.

TASK 1:

Find a place where you can spend some quiet time alone. Set these few minutes aside as sacred, where nothing or no one should disturb you. In your *Set the Captives free: 12 Studies for Individuals or Groups* Workbook, on **page 6**, you will find reflection questions, Nos. 4 and 5, which relate to *Tracking Our Past* in relation to unresolved issues. Work through these questions which will aid you in beginning to re-examine your unresolved past issues.

TASK 2:

Additionally, in this Workbook, on **pages 7 – 8**, you can now focus on **Questions 6 to 11,** to assist you in continuing to *Track the Past* as we prepare to move along on this journey.

> **"I once thought these things were valuable, but now I consider them worthless because of what the Healing Redeemer of mankind has done"** (Philippians 3:7, NLT)

2. Consistent Exercise /Physical Activities.

TASK 1:

Every lifestyle change which we adopt takes time to produce an effect. Exercise relates to **Activity,** the third component of the HEALINGS health principles. It is vital to engage in mental as well as physical movement and development. This becomes essential seeing that the mind performs well when the body undergoes regular exercise and vice versa. Be determined to start an exercise routine and keep at it. **PLAN** an exercise programme and carry it out consistently, including sessions of rigorous walking. These activities help 'flush' the mind and cause a shift in your thoughts and aid with the transformation of your thinking and bouts of anger. **REMEMBER** to enter the information on the *Emotional Healthy Lifestyle Scorecard* at the end of each Session in this Companion Workbook.

A few examples of activities are as follows:

a)jogging   b)bicycling   c)rigorous gardening   d)rigorous stretching

e)brisk walking   f)aerobics (chair-robics)   g)swimming   h)Others_____

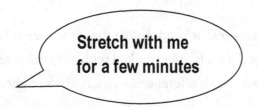

Stretch with me for a few minutes

TASK 2:

Physical exercise creates a need for **rest (lying down),** the fourth component of HEALINGS health principles. Hence ensure that you get at least seven (7) hours of sleep at night. It is during this time that the brain detoxifies itself of the toxins which are derived from negative emotions among other sources. Plan your evening well so that you put aside all activities and prepare to go to sleep at least two (2) hours before midnight.

3. The 'Before' Assessment

TASK 1:

At this time it is recommended that you take the '**Before**' Inventory of Emotional/Spiritual maturity assessment (I-E/SM), contained in the Assessments Pack.

Keeping on Track: Using the Emotional Healthy Lifestyle Scorecard

The **Emotional Healthy Lifestyle Scorecard** (see **Page 23**) includes eight (8) categories which are essential to the promotion, establishment and maintenance of your emotional well-being: Spiritual Engagement, Relationship Building, Exercise, Goal-Setting, Discussion Time, Personal Reflection, Special Reading and Water intake. A copy of the Emotional Healthy Lifestyle Scorecard appears at the end of each chapter and also in **Appendix A** at the end of this *Companion Folder*.

USE THE SCORECARD

to keep track of how you are doing on the different parts of the *Emotional Health Restoration Programme*. You can write your responses in this *Companion Folder*, or photocopy the chart. Individuals, who follow and incorporate the activities into their daily life, tend to progress faster.

For each day of the week, it is advisable that you keep an account of the amount of time spent on each activity. The activities marked with a (*) indicate that they will be ongoing during the day of each week. With reference to water, please indicate how many glasses you have consumed and for the special reading, record which verses in the Gospel of Mark you have read.

For example, the first activity on the scorecard is 'Spiritual Engagement or Personal Devotions'. You should take note of how much time you spent each day and indicate this in the space provided. Some activities require a (√) to indicate that you have been engaging in them. An example of this is the section on 'Relationship Building' and 'Discussion Time'.

4. Learn About and Practise Self-awareness

Self-awareness is about learning to better understand why you feel what you feel and why you behave in a particular way. Once you begin to understand this concept, you then have the opportunity and freedom to change things about yourself so that you can interact with other more favourably. This quality also relates to **building healthy and positive inter-personal relationships,** the fifth component of the HEALINGS health principles. By exercising your power of will, you have the option or ability to evaluate various courses of action and to select from among them. This enables you to set out the type of life that you eagerly desire to have. In order to change and become self-accepting, you need to be certain about who you are. What are your mannerisms like? What do you engage in unconsciously? Having clarity about who you are and what you want, can be empowering, thereby giving you the confidence to make changes.

Additionally, the act of developing self-awareness is important for experiencing a more fulfilling life, both at home and in various social contexts such as the classroom, place of worship and the workplace. With a better understanding of how we interact with others, we can make changes to our behaviour so that we can deal with them positively. By understanding what upset us, we can regulate and manage our self-control. Also, by understanding our weaknesses, we can learn how to manage them, and accomplish various goals despite them.

Self-awareness allows you to understand other people, how they perceive you, your attitude and your responses to others in that moment. We might quickly assume that we are self-aware, but it is helpful to have a relative scale for awareness. If you have ever been in an auto accident, you may have experienced everything happening in slow motion and noticed details of your thought processes and the event. This is a state of heightened awareness. With practice, we can learn to engage these types of heightened states and see new opportunities for interpretations in our conversations, emotions and thoughts.

TASK 1:

In an attempt to learn about and practise self-awareness, follow the instructions in each box and complete the activity.

Known Self **WRITE** two (2) things you know about yourself and that others know about you.	**Hidden Self** **LIST** two (2) things you know about yourself but that others do not know about you.
Blind Self **SHARE** with one person in the group, one (1) thing that others know about you that you do not know/ did not know.	**Unknown Self** **DISCUSS** with the group one (1) thing you did not know about yourself and no one knew either

Fig. 2: Johari's Window

EMOTIONAL TYPES AND STYLES OF RELATING

TYPE 1 (Part A)

5. Identifying Emotional Types

The filter through which you see the world, especially when you are under pressure, is your style of relating, or emotional type. On identifying your emotional type, it helps you to answer the question 'How do you deal with life's issues?' Examine the statements relating to each type below and indicate to what degree each statement relates to you. **Please try to be as tough with yourself as possible. This will help you to identify, as clearly as possible, your style of relating to others.**

0-Not At All	1-Sometimes	2-Moderately	3-Very Much		4-Definitely			
			RATINGS					
INTELLECTUAL INTENSE			**0**	**1**	**2**	**3**	**4**
1. I am bright and articulate in my speech in that I speak clearly and fluently								
2. I am a keen, insightful and discerning analyst and am most comfortable in the mind.								
3. My world is powerfully seen or examined through rational thinking.								
4. I am known for keeping my cool in heated situations.								
5. I believe I have a sad, mournful and pensive personality mainly.								
6. My sad outlook makes me usually, cautious, serious and focused.								
7. I do not trust my inner feelings about making decisions.								
8. I am slow to engage in light-hearted comedy, humorous sensual or playful activities.								
9. Whenever a difficult situation arises, I believe I can think my way through it to reach a solution.								
10. When presented with a problem, I immediately start analysing the pros and cons.								
11. In solving my problems I do not focus on how they make me feel.								
12. My over-active mind keeps me awake, hence I tend to engage in planning events rather than relying on being spontaneous.								
Other Issues								
Total for each column								

TYPE 2 (Part A)

The filter through which you see the world, especially when you are under pressure, is your style of relating, or emotional type. On identifying your emotional type, it helps you to answer the question 'How do you deal with life's issues?' Examine the statements relating to each type below and indicate to what degree each statement relates to you. **Please try to be as tough with yourself as possible. This will help you to identify, as clearly as possible, your style of relating to others.**

0-Not At All	1-Sometimes	2-Moderately	3-Very Much		4-Definitely	
			RATINGS			
THE EMPATH			**0**	**1**	**2**	**3**	**4**
1. I am highly sensitive to the various situations around me.							
2. I tend to be loving and supportive.							
3. I am a finely tuned instrument in relation to emotions.							
4. I tend to feel everything, sometimes to an extreme.							
5. Many people refer to me as being 'too emotional' or 'overly sensitive'.							
6. When my friends become upset, I also begin to feel their pain.							
7. I tend to relate to people by sensing and perceiving their true feelings.							
8. When I focus on other people's feelings, I have the ability to recognise that they run deeper than those portrayed on the surface.							
9. I believe I have a phlegmatic personality which means that I am not easily excited by actions nor easily display emotions.							
10. Based on this personality, I am unassuming, agreeable, compassionate, imaginative, calm and intuitive							
11. .I replenish my energy by being alone and I tend to become exhausted in crowds.							
12. I am sensitive to noise, smells and excessive talking.							
Other Issues							
Total for each column							

VICTOR MARSHALL

TYPE 3 (Part A)

The filter through which you see the world, especially when you are under pressure, is your style of relating, or emotional type. On identifying your emotional type, it helps you to answer the question 'How do you deal with life's issues?' Examine the statements relating to each type below and indicate to what degree each statement relates to you. **Please try to be as tough with yourself as possible. This will help you to identify, as clearly as possible, your style of relating**

0-Not At All	1-Sometimes	2-Moderately	3-Very Much		4-Definitely	
			RATINGS			
THE ROCK:			0	1	2	3	4
1. Other people consider me to be consistent, dependable and stable.							
2. They agree that I will always show up for and support them.							
3. I can express my emotions freely around others who will not get upset or judge me.							
4. I have a difficult time expressing my own feelings and my friends are always trying to get me to express my emotions.							
5. It is easier for me to listen than to share my feelings.							
6. I often feel as though I am the most dependable person among people.							
7. I am generally satisfied with the status quo in relationships, even though others try to draw me out emotionally.							
8. Practical activities are important to me and I constantly look for opportunities and always work to improve myself.							
9. I believe I have a choleric personality because I am Goal-oriented, focused, logical, though-minded.							
10. I tend to be sceptical and do not trust easily. Therefore, I need to investigate the facts on my own and then analyse them.							
11. I have a great sense of autonomy and independence and I tend to be highly competitive.							
12. My problem-solving skills are well developed. As long as I am satisfied with reasoning behind my strategy, I act boldly and self-confidently.							
Other Issues							
Total for each column							

TYPE 4 (Part A)

The filter through which you see the world, especially when you are under pressure, is your style of relating, or emotional type. On identifying your emotional type, it helps you to answer the question 'How do you deal with life's issues?' Examine the statements relating to each type below and indicate to what degree each statement relates to you. **Please try to be as tough with yourself as possible. This will help you to identify, as clearly as possible, your style of relating**

0-Not At All	1-Sometimes	2-Moderately	3-Very Much		4-Definitely		
				RATINGS			
ATTUNED TO EMOTIONS			0	1	2	3	4
1. I am in touch with my emotions and am not afraid to share them.							
2. I usually possess high amounts of energy, and tend to be restless and spontaneous.							
3. I tend to be buoyant and lively. I can quickly process a negative situation or issue and move on. This shows that I am optimistic.							
4. My weakness is that I tend to share 'too much information' and this 'over-sharing can cause others to experience 'burn out'.							
5. I become anxious if I keep my feelings stored inside continuously.							
6. Chemical imbalances, addictions and mood disorders tend to affect my emotional wellbeing							
7. Often times, I feel bored if I am not absorbed by something intriguing.							
8. My constant cravings for adventure and novelty are the major motivating force behind my actions, decisions and choices.							
9. I believe I have a sanguine personality because I am autonomous, creative, curious, impulsive and unconventional.							
10. My personality encourages me to prefer spontaneity and moments of intellectual discovery.							
11. When a problem arises, my first impulse is to pick up the telephone and share the issue with a close person.							
12. I find it difficult to identify or understand other people's emotional boundaries.							
Other Issues							
Total for each column							

Indicating and Analysing the Score

Category of Emotional Type	Scores			
	0 – 12	13 – 24	25 - 36	37 – 48
	Level of Relating Emotionally			
	Mildly	Partially	Moderately	Definitely
Intellectual: Intense Thinker				
Empath: Emotional Sponge				
Rock: Strong and Silent				
Gusher: Attuned to Emotions				

Instructions: After identifying your emotional type, place the number for each rating on the dotted lines in brackets, multiply the number in the brackets and then ADD all sub-totals to arrive at a **FINAL TOTAL** for each category of emotional type. Afterwards, tick the scoring range in the chart above into which your final total fit.

EXAMPLE: $\quad 0 \quad + \quad 3 \quad + \quad 2 \quad + \quad 9 \quad + \quad 4 \quad = \quad 18$

$\qquad\qquad (0 \times 2) \quad + \quad (1\times3) \quad + \quad (2\times1) \quad + \quad (3\times3) \quad + \quad (4\times1) \quad =$

This score of 18 falls in the second level of relating emotionally in the chart above.

YOUR SCORES:

The Gusher: $(0 \times ...) \quad + \quad (1 \times ...) \quad + \quad (2 \times ...) \quad + \quad (3 \times ...) \quad + \quad (4 \times ....) \quad =$

Profile on Your Emotional Type/Style of Relating Emotionally		
Category of Emotional Type	Total Score	Level of Relating Emotionally
Intellectual: Intense Thinker		
Empath: Emotional Sponge		
Rock: Strong and Silent		
Gusher: Attuned to Emotions		

NB: The category with the highest score is your emotional type.

SOURCE: This tool, which gauges your style of relating emotionally, was designed using basic information from Judith Orloff, *Emotional Freedom: Liberate Yourself from Negative Emotions and Transform Your Life* (NY: Harmony Books, 2009), p. 99.

Personal Reflective Study Session (WEEK 1)

- What has the first session done for you in relation to your emotional wellbeing and spiritual maturity?

....

....

....

....

- How eager are you to experience emotional and spiritual progress?

....

....

....

....

- What benefits did you gain from completing the inventory of emotional/spiritual maturity?

....

....

....

....

- Identify one (1) new idea, thought or new insight you have learnt from this first session

....

....

....

....

Emotional Health Lifestyle Scorecard

Week _____

ACTIVITY	DAY OF THE WEEK AND DATE						
	Sun ----/----/----	Mon ----/----/----	Tues ----/----/----	Wed ----/----/----	Thurs ----/----/----	Fri ----/----/----	Sat ----/----/----
Spiritual Engagement * Prepare for the journey of restoration with spiritual practices (See *Set the Captives Free Workbook*, pp.15, 73							
Relationship Building Pray for a particular family member/relative/ friend with whom you are having difficulty							
Exercise Engage in Exercise. State the type and amount of time daily							
Goal-setting Identify two or three things you wish to accomplish daily AND MONTHLY. This inspires hope and optimism in that you would have accomplished a goal							
Discussion Time * Identify any two (2) issues to be addressed with a particular family member/relative/friend, and prayerfully talk to that person about the issues							
Personal Reflection How much time have you spent on the reflection activity at the end of each **SESSION**?							
Special Reading On a daily basis, read ten (10) verses from the Gospel of St Mark 1-12. Also identify and **MEMORISE** the verse that attracts you.	*Verses Read*	*Verses Read*	*Verses Read*	*Verses Read*	*Verses Read*	*Verses Read*	*Verses Read*
.... *Favourite Verse(s)*	....	....	....	....	....	....	....
Water How many glasses of water did you drink during the day?							

NOTE: * Place a tick (√) in the box next to these items to show that you have completed the activity on a daily basis. It is expected that these activities will take time and will be on-going.

NOTES

Feel free to use this space to write out the verse/ thought you are memorising from the chapter you have read this week, as a way of helping you internalise the information.

Session Two

Gauging Your Degree of Emotional Wounded-ness

During this session, pay attention to:

1) Social factors which contribute to emotional instability.

2) The impact of emotional distress on your well-being

3) The features relating to the degree of emotional wounded-ness

4) Whether you make use of the Sacred Text to aid you on your journey.

You will notice in this *Companion Folder* that you have the outline of the PowerPoint presentation for **Session Two** so that you may follow along.

DVD/PowerPoint Slides

Session Two

Gauging Your Degree of Emotional Wounded-ness

During the PowerPoint presentations, feel free to follow along with the slides that correspond with those in the session. You can fill in the blank spaces with the missing words. Use the blanks in the margin with the letters that match to the letters on the blanks in the PowerPoint slides. (For example, for blank [e2], write the answer on the line next to the section of the slide marked [e2].

1.

> # EMOTIONAL HEALTH RESTORATION PROGRAMME
>
> Identifying Emotional Dys-functionality and Possible Solutions

2.

> ## Session 2
>
> Gauging Your Degree of Emotional Wounded-ness

Factors Contributing to Difficulties

Various social factors can impact negatively on us as individuals or as a family. Some of these are compulsive activities (Gambling etc), _____a_____ due to death of a very close person, long-term health conditions, ____b____ social isolation, loneliness, substance addictions (drugs, etc), traumas, unemployment, violence.

Individuals respond to life's difficulties and struggles differently. A stressful and adverse situation can emerge because of family or relationship problems, ____c____ setbacks, health problems, or workplace challenges among others. This indicates that we can be influenced (*positively or negatively*) by our social environment.

Monroe, S. M., Slavich, G. M., Georgiades, K. (2009). The Social Environment and life stress in depression'. In I. H. Gotlib & C. L. Hammen (eds), *Handbook of Depression,* 2nd edn (NY: The Guildford Press), 340- 360 (341).

The Twelve 'Risk' Categories

1. Emotional Instability
2. **Emotional Hurt**
3. Lifestyle
4. Nutrition
5. Forgiveness
6. Abuse
7. Unresolved Issues
8. Inability to Cope
9. Medical Condition
10. Childhood Adversity
11. Psychological Needs
12. Mental Functioning

3.

a. _____

b. _____

4.

c. _____

5.

Risk 2: Emotional Hurt

Different emotional responses such as anger, fear or sadness tend to emerge because of the negative impact of these social issues. They can emerge in the form of unwelcome or _____d_____ changes to circumstances in one's life. Individuals who experience such severe difficulties tend to be emotionally distressed.

6.

d. _____

Risk Factors for Emotional Distress

Every day testifies to the increase of insanity, murder, and suicide. … Everywhere there are hearts crying out for something which they have not. They long for a power that will give them mastery over [*evil practices*], a power that will deliver them from the bondage of evil, a power that will give health and life and peace. The world needs today what it needed nineteen hundred years ago—a revelation of [*The Healing Redeemer*]. A great work of reform is demanded, and it is only through the grace of [*The Almighty Healing Redeemer*] that the work of restoration (e.g: physical, mental, and spiritual) can be accomplished.

White, E. G. (1905). *Ministry of Healing* (Hagerstown, MD: Review and Herald Publishing Association, p.143.

7.

Emotional Distress Defined

Emotional distress can occur when individuals:

- experience ___e___ disturbance such as anxiety,

- display negative emotions and

- become easily bothered.

Thomas, V. and Godfrey, S. (2018). Understanding water-related emotional distress for improving water services: a case study from an Ethiopian small town. *Journal of Water, Sanitation and Hygiene for Development*, 8 (2), 196–207 (197); Yusuf, A.J. Yusuf, Nuhu, F. T., and Olisah, V. O. (2013). Emotional distress among caregivers of patients with epilepsy in Katsina State, Northern Nigeria. *African Journal of Psychiatry*, 16 (1), 41-44 (41).

8.

e. _____

Contributory Factors to Emotional Distress

A number of factors were identified which can either cause or contribute to emotional distress. From the research,

- familial issues, emotional problems

- clinical problems and

- _____**f**_____ difficulties increased the risk of emotional distress.

Saeedi-Saedi H, Shahidsales S, Koochak-Pour M, Sabahi E, Moridi I. (2015). Evaluation of emotional distress in breast cancer patients. *Iranian Journal of Cancer Prevention*, 8 (1), 36-41m(38).

9.

f. _____

Emotional Wounded-ness

When a person experiences an emotional hurt, it means that his/her emotional _____**g**_____ could be dented or disturbed deeply, thereby causing a level of _____**h**_____. Such a person can be affected emotionally in one of four different degrees of wounded-ness: bruised, broken, damaged and wounded. They range from deeply affected to being least affected.

Marshall, V. D. (2015) *On the Road to Forgiveness: Experiencing Healing on the Way (*IN: AuthorHouse), pp. 92-93.

10.

g. _____

h. _____

Degree of Emotional Wounded-ness

Deeply/Profoundly Affected | Severely Affected | Moderately Affected | Least Affected

Broken · Whole

11.

i. _____

j. _____

k. _____

Impact of Emotional Wounded-ness On Functionality

A person's degree of emotional woundedness tends to be an indicator of his/her level of ___l___, where individuals may display a poor level such as dysfunctionality or a high level, such as being functional. The other levels are ___m___, and non-functional. Individuals, who are ___o___ and deeply/profoundly affected emotionally, tend to be dysfunctional or non-functional.

Marshall, *On the Road to Forgiveness,* p.93.

12.

l. _____

m. _____

o. _____

Dys-functionality

Dysfunctionality is an abnormal functioning. It refers to an *unhealthy* interpersonal behaviour, *persistent negative* attitude or unwholesome interaction with an individual or a group. This abnormal state can bring about a surface-level or deep impact. A deep impact can cause a high level of emotional wounded-ness which can contribute to one's emotional im-maturity.

13.

The Emotionally Bruised

Emotionally bruised individuals carry slight emotional pain which produces a sense of ___p___, one of the primary negative emotions. This category of emotionally wounded people tends to withdraw from others and are afraid to be open or to interact with others. Psychologically, there is a ____q____ on their emotional stability and inter-personal relationships. However, they are functional, to the extent that they can conduct socially-assigned tasks without professional or social support.

Marshall, *On the Road to Forgiveness,* pp. 92, 222.

14.

p. _____

q. _____

Elements of Functionality

In a research study of 56 Grade 6 Chinese primary school children, researchers assessed their experience of being offended and hurt by peers or siblings and their level of forgiveness for the offenders. The children were hurt because of _____r____, being treated unfairly, or being teased by peers, but not bullied. All indicated that they were unable to _____s_____ the offender at the time.

Huia, E. K. P. and Chau T. S. (2009). The impact of a forgiveness intervention with Hong Kong Chinese children hurt in interpersonal relationships. *British Journal of Guidance and Counselling*, 37 (2), 141-156 (144).

15.

r. _____

s. _____

Effect of Forgiveness on Wellbeing

The children in the study of Huia and Chau, who extended forgiveness:

- experienced a significant decrease in _____t_____

- obtain an increase in _____u_____ and hope and

- were more _____v_____, happier and at peace.

Huia, and Chau, 'The impact of a forgiveness intervention with Hong Kong Chinese children hurt in interpersonal relationships', p.144.

16.

t. _____

u. _____

v. _____

Characteristics of the Emotional Wounded

The type of experiences which bring emotional and physical _____w_____ indicate that a person's emotional _____x_____ has been pierced intensely, a feature of being emotionally wounded.

Marshall, *On the Road to Forgiveness*, pp. 92-93.

17.

w. _____

x. _____

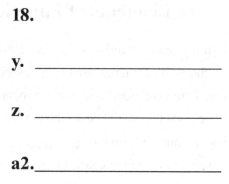

Characteristics of the Emotional Wounded

In a study of 1500 pregnant women who experience _____y_____ violence, they were exposed predominantly to:

- ____z_____ violence, along with
- physical and sexual violence. This experience positioned them to be _____a2_____of emotional distress.

Groves, A. K., Kagee, A., Maman, S., Moodley, D., & Rouse, P. (2012). Associations Between Intimate Partner Violence and Emotional Distress Among Pregnant Women in Durban, South Africa. *Journal of Interpersonal Violence*, 27(7), 1341-1356; Marshall, *On the Road to Forgiveness,* p.93.

18.

y. _____

z. _____

a2._____

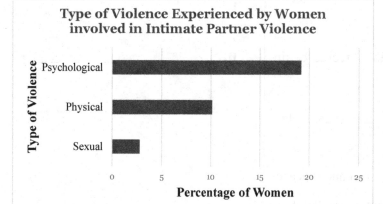

Type of Violence Experienced by Women involved in Intimate Partner Violence

19.

Characteristics of the Emotionally Wounded

The women had social ____ g2_____which did not positively impact on violence during pregnancy, but contributed to emotional distress. It acted as a buffer, suggesting that the impact was moderate as opposed to severe or profound. These symptomatic features are indicative of being emotionally wounded.

20.

b2._____

___j2___Emotionally Hurt

Emotionally broken individuals fall into this category and experience ___c2___ difficulties in seeking to mend from their wounded-ness.

21.

c2._____

Emotionally broken individuals are affected by ___d2___ disorders such as depression, mood and personality disorders, resulting in them lacking a sense of belonging, and a decrease in social interaction. Such experiences contribute to them being ___e2___ dysfunctional, which negatively impacts on their emotional and psychological wellbeing.

22.

d2._____

e2._____

Profound Emotional Hurt

Individuals who are emotionally hurt to a profound degree experience psychological issues in areas such as coping, and tend to use maladaptive strategies predominantly. Difficulties arise in terms of social, ___f2___. Emotionally damaged individuals tend to

- Experience impairment of value

- Undergo a reduction in ___g2___, and

- Be unable to function normally,

thereby leading to social dysfunctionality.

23.

f2._____

g2._____

Stefano Porcelli, S., van der Wee, N., van der Werff, S., Aghajani, M., Glennon, J. C., van Heukelum, S., Mogavero, f. et al. (2019). Social brain, social dysfunction and social withdrawal. *Neuroscience & Bio-behavioral Reviews*, 97, 10-33 (11).

Functional Behaviour of the Emotionally Damaged

Emotionally-damaged individuals struggle to carry out daily tasks and fulfil various roles because of the chronic disorganization of family members. Evidence of this is in disturbed family dynamics or relationships because of various types of _____**h2**_____ be it emotional, physical or substance.

Lynda Juall Carpenito-Moyet, *Handbook of Nursing Diagnosis* (Philadelphia, PA: Lippincott Williams & Wilkins, 11th edn, 2006, p. 150.

Evidence

Individuals' dysfunctionality or non-functionality is related to levels of _____**i2**_____ and depression. In a study conducted with 175 female patients diagnosed with Chronic Pelvic Pain.

- more than 75% of them was in ___**j2**_____ for more than 2 years.
- 77% of them presented with mild to severe levels of anxiety, and
- 53.5% experienced mild to severe _____**k2**_____.

Bryant, C., Cockburn, R., Plante, A., & Chia, A. (2016). The psychological profile of women presenting to a multidisciplinary clinic for chronic pelvic pain: high levels of psychological dysfunction and implications for practice. *Journal of Pain Research*, 9, 1049-1056 (1052).

Spiritual Resources for the Emotionally Hurt

The _____**l2**_____ which Christ diffuses through the whole being is a vitalizing power. Every vital part—the brain, the heart, the nerves—it touches with healing. By it, the highest energies of the being are aroused to activity. It frees the soul from the guilt and sorrow, the anxiety and care, that crush the life forces. With it come serenity and composure. It implants in the soul, joy that nothing earthly can destroy,—joy in the Holy Spirit,—health-giving, life-giving joy.

White, E. G. (1905). *Ministry of Healing* (Hagerstown, MD: Review and Herald Publishing Association, p.115.

24.

h2._____

25.

i2._____

j2._____

k2._____

26.

l2._____

Developing Positive Mindset for Wellbeing

Courage, _____**m2**_____, faith, sympathy, love, promote health and prolong life. A contented mind, a cheerful spirit, is health to the body and strength to the soul. "A merry [rejoicing] heart doeth good like a medicine"(Proverbs 17:22).

White, E. G. (1905). *Ministry of Healing* (Hagerstown MD: Review and Herald Publishing Association, p.241.

Ancient Counsel

The various degrees of emotional hurt could lead to some type of illness, be it a physical or psychological. Individuals who become ill can admit that their 'heart is overwhelmed' and _____**n2**_____with the Divine Creator to 'lead me to the Rock that is higher than I' (Psalm 61:2). It is in this Rock, that you can sense a time of peace while you face sudden or unexpected ill-health.

Positive Recommendation

In all that we engage in and interact with, we are reminded to

Bless the Lord, O my soul,
    and forget not all his benefits,
We do not need to carry on living with our
broken-ness or wounded-ness because we can
look to, call upon the Almighty Healer "who
forgives all your iniquity,
    who _____**o2**_____ all your diseases".
(Psalm 103:2-3, NKJV)

27.

m2._____

28.

n2._____

29.

o2._____

Summary

- Experiencing life's struggles makes it difficult to cope with the complex social environment.
- Individuals who experience emotional distress tend to experience mood disturbance such as depression, display negative emotions such as fear and become easily bothered.
- A person's degree of emotional wounded-ness is indicative of his/her level of functionality.
- Reading, meditating on and studying the inspirational and Sacred Text aid in improving emotional well-being.

Insightful Perspectives

> **a)** Turn to Chapter 6 in in *Set the Captives Free (Resource Guide)*, **pages 30-32** and read the sub-section entitled 'Processes'.
>
> **b)** Remember to read Chapter 2 'Facing our Open Wounds' in *Raising the Wounded: Grasping for Hope in the Midst of Despair.*

Emotional Healthy Lifestyle Matters

Let's turn to the *emotional healthy lifestyle matters* section. These are activities and tasks we can engage in to aid our emotional, physical, psychological, relational, social and spiritual development. Some of these can be done on your own at home.

1. De-clutter Emotionally to Begin the Healing Process

The term de-clutter refers to the act of removing complications, disorder, mess or un-necessary matter from your life. It also refers to organising and prioritising mental thoughts. It is important to make a decision on the memories and mental images we carry around in your mind. This activity relates to your internal **Environment,** the second component of the HEALINGS health principles. Your memories and mental thoughts are part of the emotional environment which is played out at home, on the playground or in the workplace. If these mental images and thoughts do not impact on you positively, but instead, cause you pain, this is an indication that you need to get rid of them.

TASK 1: (See Appendix B)

One effective way to de-clutter is to engage in expressive writing of **the negative or unresolved issue.** Write out the issue over 3 days and spend about 10 – 15 minutes each time.

       GUIDELINES: Write out your very deepest thoughts and feeling *(which are hidden and unknown to others).* Try to let go, be free and explore an extremely important emotional issue that has affected you and your life. You may tie your topic to your relationships with others, including parents, lovers, friends, or relatives; to your past, your present, or your future; or to who you have been, who you would like to be, or who you are now. You may write about the same general issues or experiences on all the days of writing or on different topics each day. All of your writing will be completely confidential. Don't worry about spelling, sentence structure, or grammar. The only rule is that once you begin writing, continue to do so until your time is up. Afterwards, burn it and resolve that you will not go back to the issue, having reached this stage of the programme. This physical act of burning the paper helps you clear your mind of the issue, thereby beginning the de-cluttering process.

TASK 2:

Your *Set the Captives free: 12 Studies for Individuals or Groups* Workbook, on **pages 10-14**, has activities to assist you in addressing specific issues in Emotional Healing. Work through **Questions 1 – 9** as you seek to address the emotional issues.

2. Therapeutic Evaluation

TASK 1:

This task requires you to analyse the different facets of your emotional being up to this point by making a comparison between these areas. Having completed the assessment tools so far, write your **(a)** degree of emotional wounded-ness, **(b)**level of emotional/spiritual maturity in the spaces below: **(a)**_____ **(b)**_____

Review your profile on relating emotionally by looking at **page 21** in this *Companion Folder*. My emotional type is _____.

How are these three aspects of your emotional well-being related?

_____

_____

_____

3. Practising and Developing Self Awareness (To be completed at home)

Over the next week, find a quiet place and engage in the following activity with classical or Gospel music.

a) Identify two (2) values you hold dearly? Eg. Honesty

_____

_____

b) What is your major philosophy in life?

_____

_____

c) How do you normally react when someone close to you tells you off OR criticises you?

_____

_____

d) How do you normally react when someone at your workplace/ college/ church/ university/ club tells you off OR criticises you?

_____

_____

e) Share two (2) things you do unconsciously, but require someone to alert you about them. For example, **You do not look at a person when speaking to him/her; you speak too quickly.**

_____

_____

f) Share ONE (1) rule which you live by daily? Eg. **I will not be late.**

_____

_____

g) How positive is your attitude towards people in general? Please rate it on the scale below.

Not Positive					Positive					Very Positive
0	1	2	3	4	5	6	7	8	9	10

h) Give a copy of this sheet to **two (2) separate** individuals who know you very well. Ask each of them to fill it out and return it to you. Afterwards, compare your list with your friends' lists.

i) Having compared the three (3) lists, would you say that you unconsciously do some of the things on your friends' list? Write down TWO (2) things you plan to carry out to revise your reactions and attitudes? **E.g:** Developing new thoughts about various life's situations.

_____

_____

_____

_____

_____

_____

_____

_____

_____

_____

_____

_____

_____

_____

_____

Have you distributed the Self-awareness forms to

TWO INDIVIDUALS?

4) Replacing Negative Views/Thoughts with Inspiring Material.

TASK 1:

(a) Take a look at the following verse below and **READ** it **affirmatively** to a group member.

"Therefore, [there is] now no condemnation (no adjudging guilty of wrong) for those who are in Christ Jesus, who live [and] walk not after the dictates of the flesh, but after the dictates of the Spirit" (Rom 8:1, AMP).

(b) Complete the missing words, memorize and then recite it a few times to a group member.

"For God did not give us a spirit of _____ (of cowardice, of craven and cringing and fawning fear), but [He has given us a spirit] of power and of love and of a _____ mind *and* discipline *and* self-control" (2 Tim 1:7, AMP).

c) Which of these texts attract your attention the most? Why?

_____

_____

_____

_____

_____

5) Water Intake

As part of the HEALINGS health principles on which this *Emotional Health Restoration Programme* is based, water is a key element in the **Nutrition** strand. Even when we have a balanced diet and our water intake is low, this can negatively affect the functioning of the organs in the body. Additionally, remember that your body weight is approximately 60 percent water. All of your cells, organs, and tissues need water to help regulate their temperature and maintain other bodily functions. Since your body loses water through breathing, sweating, and digestion, it is essential to maintain your high intake of water to re-hydrate the body.

TASK 1:

Attempt to spread your eight (8) glasses of water between your three (3) meals of the day. First, make an effort to have two (2) glasses of water as soon as you rise on mornings; have 2 glasses before breakfast, two before lunch, and two before supper.

> **CHALLENGE:** During this WEEK, as soon as you rise from bed every morning, **take TWO (2) glasses of warm water.** Do this just before you begin your devotions. While you move around in the kitchen, take another glass of water at room temperature. This would help you to have your three (3) glasses of water before your first meal of the day.

6. Assessment

Turn to the Assessment and Evaluation Tools Kit and complete the **Self-awareness Questionnaire (SAQ 3) – Assertive Behaviour**. Also, take some time to complete the **Spiritual Self-care and Wellness Assessment** relating to your spiritual wellness. As you work through the statements, seek to be as honest as possible and be very demanding on yourself.

Personal Reflection (WEEK 2)

Reflectively study the text below.

> O [Holy One], listen to my cry!
>> Hear my prayer!
> ² From the ends of the earth,
>> I cry to you for help
>> when my heart is overwhelmed.
>> Lead me to the towering rock of safety,
> ³ for you are my safe refuge,
>> a fortress where my enemies cannot reach me.
> ⁴ Let me live forever in your sanctuary,
>> safe beneath the shelter of your wings!

_____ (Psalm 61:1-4, NLT)

- Which verse attracts your attention? (**Write it below**)

_____

_____

_____

_____

- Write down any insights you have gained from these verses.

_____

_____

_____

- How has these verses helped you emotionally?

_____

_____

_____

- What emotions such as feelings or moods do the verses bring out? **(E.g loneliness)** Which of these are you experiencing now / have experienced in the last month?

_____

_____

_____

_____

_____

_____

- Which major (main) idea or clause or significant word(s) is/ are repeated more than two (2) times in the verses above?

_____

_____

_____

_____

_____

_____

_____

- Reflect on these major ideas/ clauses or significant words and **write down/ share** what these ideas have done for you.

_____

_____

_____

_____

_____

_____

Emotional Health Lifestyle Scorecard

Week _____

ACTIVITY	DAY OF THE WEEK AND DATE						
	Sun ----/----/----	Mon ----/----/----	Tues ----/----/----	Wed ----/----/----	Thurs ----/----/----	Fri ----/----/----	Sat ----/----/----
Spiritual Engagement * Prepare for the journey of restoration with spiritual practices (See *Set the Captives Free Workbook*, pp.15, 73							
Relationship Building Pray for a particular family member/relative/ friend with whom you are having difficulty							
Exercise Engage in Exercise. State the type and amount of time daily							
Goal-setting Identify two or three things you wish to accomplish daily AND MONTHLY. This inspires hope and optimism in that you would have accomplished a goal							
Discussion Time * Identify any two (2) issues to be addressed with a particular family member/relative/friend, and prayerfully talk to that person about the issues							
Personal Reflection How much time have you spent on the reflection activity at the end of each **SESSION**?							
Special Reading On a daily basis, read ten (10) verses from the Gospel of St Mark 1-12. Also identify and **MEMORISE** the verse that attracts you. .... *Favourite Verse(s)*	*Verses Read*	*Verses Read*	*Verses Read*	*Verses Read*	*Verses Read*	*Verses Read*	*Verses Read* ....
Water How many glasses of water did you drink during the day?							

NOTE: * Place a tick (√) in the box next to these items to show that you have completed the activity on a daily basis. It is expected that these activities will take time and will be on-going.

NOTES

Feel free to use this space to write out the verse you are memorising from the chapter you have read this week, as a way of helping you internalise the text.

Session Three

Lifestyle Interventions for Emotional Ill-health

During this session, pay attention to:

1) The eight (8) inter-related **HEALINGS** health principles.

2) The importance of being optimistic and setting realistic goals.

3) How **sleep detox** can enhance your emotional well-being

4) Why emotionally distressed individuals benefit from **regular physical exercise.**

You will notice in your workbook that you have the outline of the PowerPoint presentation for **Session Three**, so that you may follow along.

DVD/PowerPoint Slides

Session Three

Lifestyle Intervention for Emotional Ill-health

During the PowerPoint presentations, feel free to follow along with the slides that correspond with those in the session. You can fill in the blank spaces with the missing words. Use the blanks in the margin with the letters that match to the letters on the blanks in the PowerPoint slides. (For example, for blank [h2], write the answer on the line next to the section of the slide marked [h2].

1.

> # EMOTIONAL HEALTH RESTORATION PROGRAMME
>
> Identifying Emotional Dys-functionality and Possible Solutions

2.

> # Session 3
>
> ## Lifestyle Intervention for Emotional Ill-health

The Twelve 'Risk' Categories

1. Emotional Instability
2. Emotional Hurt
3. **Lifestyle**
4. Nutrition
5. Forgiveness
6. Abuse
7. Unresolved Issues
8. Inability to Cope
9. Medical Condition
10. Childhood Adversity
11. Psychological Needs
12. Mental Functioning

3.

The Risks Categories

The lifestyle intervention recommended in this Session can positively impact your emotional well-being. The following non-modifiable factors contribute to Childhood adversity:

environmental factors, ___**a**___ history, genetic input, socialisation process, and

trans-generational issues. Various forms of abuse are also non-modifiable. The other 10 risks can be modified so that you can experience some degree of healing.

4.

a. _____

The HEALINGS Health Principles

The lifestyle intervention is based on 8 elements:

a) **H**ope /optimism
b) **E**xercise/Physical Activity
c) **A**tmosphere (internal and external environment)
d) **L**ying down (Rest)
e) **I**nter-personal Relationships
f) **N**utrition
g) Spiritual **G**uidance
h) **S**unlight

5.

Philosophy of HEALINGS
Health Principles

Individuals make choices about their health, supported by evidence-based ___b___. The central belief of this philosophy is that the 8 principles are inter-related. In order for individuals to achieve _____c_____ health, all 8 principles should be adopted, implemented and maintained.

6.

b. _____

c. _____

Stimulate Hope

Individuals need hope which relates to optimism, and which also generates positive expectations. When there is optimism, individuals have the ____d_____ to use goal-acquisition _____e_____ which help them pursue such goals successfully in spite of possible challenges.

Kardas, F., Cam, Z., Eskısu, M. & Gelıbolu, S. (2019). Gratitude, Hope, Optimism and Life Satisfaction as Predictors of Psychological Well-Being. *Eurasian Journal of Educational Research*, 19 (82), 81-100 (83, 84).

7.

d. _____

e. _____

Stimulate Hope

Researchers at four Turkish public universities conducted a study with a total of 510 university students, aged 17 to 30, to determine whether or not gratitude, hope, optimism and life satisfaction are predictors of psychological well-Being. The study showed that hope was the second most predictive variable after gratitude as a determinant of positive psychological well-being.

Kardas et al., Gratitude, Hope, Optimism and Life Satisfaction as Predictors of. Psychological Well-Being, p.91.

8.

Hope for the Terminally ill

Furthermore, hope, as a basic quality of human beings, is essential for patients diagnosed with chronic diseases such as Alzheimer's disease, cancer and cardio-vascular disease, especially when it is terminal. The diagnosis often hinders the ___f___ of personal, professional and other goals. Such barriers to patients' achievements in life can create frustration, thereby triggering negative emotions such as anger, sadness and regret.

Baczewska, B., Block, B., Kropornicka, B., Niedzielski, A., Malm, M., Zwolak, A., and Makara-Studzińska, M. (2019). Hope in Hospitalized Patients with Terminal Cancer. *International Journal of Environmental Research and Public Health*, 16(20), 3867.

Regular Physical Exercise

Another lifestyle intervention is regular physical exercise. This comes in the form of :
- ___g___ such as brisk walking
- Bone-strengthening (e.g: push-ups)
- Muscle-strengthening and
- Stretching activities

World Health Organisation Recommendation

Adults, age 18-64, engage in 150–300 minutes of moderate-intense aerobic physical activity; or 75–150 minutes of vigorous-intense aerobic physical activity per week. It should include muscle-strengthening activities on 2 or more days a week. Meanwhile, adults age 65+, along with the above, should also include multi-component physical activities, emphasizing _____h_____ balance and strength training at moderate or greater intensity, on 3 or more days a week. This promotes functional capacity and prevent falls.

9.

f. _____

10.

g. _____

11.

h. _____

Physical Exercise Improves Psychological Health

80 male and female, in the 18-58 age range, were involved in a Harvard study, comparing the impact of aerobic exercise with physical stretching on the way they respond to their emotions. Results indicate that the aerobic group:
- reported less emotional difficulties such as sadness and _____i_____than the stretching group.
- displayed _____j_____ during initial difficulties better than the group which stretched.

Bernstein, E. E. & McNally, R. J. (2016). Acute aerobic exercise helps overcome emotion regulation deficits. *Cognition and Emotion,* 31 (4), pp. 834-843.

12.

i. _____

j. _____

Create a Conducive Atmosphere

Research shows that parents, who instil the importance and value of education in their children and help them with future educational plans, and who are involved in their school's activities, are establishing an environment which ____k_____ children's positive mental health. Consequently, the children are motivated to engage in academic work, both behaviourally and emotionally.

Ming-Te Wang, M., & Sheikh-Khalil, S. (2014). Does Parental Involvement Matter for Student Achievement and Mental Health in High School? *Child Development* 85 (2), pp.610-625 (620).

13.

k. _____

Supportive Home Environment

When there is disagreement between father and mother, the children partake of the same spirit. Make your home atmosphere fragrant with tender thoughtfulness. ...The traits of character you cherish in life will not be changed by death or by the resurrection. You will come up from the grave with the same disposition you manifested in your home and in society. Christ, *The Healing Messiah,* does not change the character at His coming. The work of transformation must be done now. Our daily lives are determining our destiny.

White, E. G. (1952). *Adventist Home* (Nashville: Southern Publishing), p.16.

14.

Sleep Detox

Sleep is a state of immobility with greatly reduced responsiveness to the environment or stimuli. It is fundamental for neuronal detoxification, tissue ____ l____, conservation of ____m____, enhancement of the immune system, memory consolidation, and emotion regulation.

Siegel, J. Clues to the functions of mammalian sleep. *Nature* **437**, 1264–1271 (2005); Zaccaro A., Conversano C., Lai E., Gemignani A. (2019) Relationship Between Emotions, Sleep and Well-Being. In Pingitore A., Mastorci F., Vassalle C. (eds) *Adolescent Health and Wellbeing*. Switzerland: Springer), 153-166 (153,154).

15.

l. _____

m. _____

Effects of Sleep Deprivation

Research involving 1,125 American students, age 17-24, with 63% being females, indicated that sleep deprivation led to greater negative mood such as anger, confusion, depression, fatigue, and ____ n____, higher levels of stress, more physical illnesses, substance abuse (e. g: alcohol, drugs) and ____o____ medication.

Lund, H. G., Reider, B. D. , Whiting, A. B., & Prichard, J. R. (2010). Sleep Patterns and Predictors of Disturbed Sleep in a Large Population of College Students. *Journal of Adolescent Health*, 46 (2), pp.124-132 (128).

16.

n. _____

o. _____

Insightful Counsel

God designs that the Sabbath shall direct the minds of men to the contemplation of His created works. Nature speaks to their senses, declaring that there is a living God, the Creator, the Supreme Ruler of all. "The heavens declare the glory of God; and the firmament showeth His handiwork. Day unto day uttereth speech, and night unto night showeth knowledge." Psalm 19:1, 2. The beauty that clothes the earth is a token of God's love. We may behold it in the everlasting hills, in the lofty trees, in the opening buds and the delicate flowers. All speak to us of God. The Sabbath, ever pointing to Him who made them all, bids men open the great book of nature and trace therein the wisdom, the power, and the love of the Creator.

White, E. G. (1890). *Patriarchs and Prophets* (Mountain View, CA: Pacific Press Publishing Association, pp.47-48.

17.

Get Connected

553 Polish university students were studied in two groups.
- Partners in nonmarital _____**p**_____ relationships reported greater overall social support than single people.
- _____**q**_____social support was negatively associated with anxiety and depression and positively linked with psychological (e.g: positive functioning in life) and emotional well-being (e.g: positive feeling).

Adamczyk, K. & Segrin, C. (2014). Perceived Social Support and Mental Health Among Single vs. Partnered Polish Young Adults. *Current Psychology*, 34, 82-96 (91).

Insightful Guidance

It is natural to seek companionship. Everyone will find companions or make them. And just in proportion to the strength of the friendship will be the amount of influence which friends will exert over one another for good or for evil. All will have associates and will influence and be influenced in their turn. The Lord, [*Almighty Healer of all diseases*] formed man for _____**r**_____, and He designs that we shall be imbued with the kind, loving nature of Christ and shall through association be bound together in close relationship as children of God, doing work for time and for eternity.

White, E. G. (2000). *Mind, Character & Personality Vol. 2* (Hagerstown, MD: Review & Herald Publishing Association), p.609.

Wholesome and Balanced Diet

Every meal should consist of nutrient-dense, whole-grain bread and cereals. Macro-nutrients are needed in terms of carbohydrates which supply energy, protein for tissue growth and repair and fats needed for energy, _____**s**____ and protection. Micro-nutrients such as vitamins are 'protective foods' for building up the immune system, while minerals are for healthy bones and growth.

18.

p. _____

q. _____

19.

r. _____

20.

s. _____

Food Groups

Fruit and vegetables consumption provide a concentration of:

- primarily vitamins A and C;
- minerals such as electrolytes; and
- phyto-chemicals and anti-oxidants such as lycopene.

Various compounds such as dietary fibre and folic acid have been linked to lower incidence of chronic diseases such as cancers seeing that they act as _____**t**_____ components.

Joanne L. Slavin, Beate Lloyd, Health Benefits of Fruits and Vegetables, *Advances in Nutrition*, Volume 3, Issue 4, July 2012, pp.506–516 (511).

21.

t. _____

Explore Spiritual Guidance

On taking a holistic view of patients who have been diagnosed with a chronic disease, the strategy includes physical and psycho-social treatment, with the ____**u**____ dimension being added to complete the holistic perspective. Research indicates that spirituality and religiosity:

- assist in providing better quality of life,
- contribute to positive self-care and
- enhance self-esteem.

Abu, H.O., Ulbricht, C., Ding, E., Allison, J. J., Salmoirago-Blotcher, E., Goldberg, R. J., Kiefe I. C. (2018). Association of religiosity and spirituality with quality of life in patients with cardiovascular disease: a systematic review. *Quality of Life Research, 27*, 2777–2797.

22.

u. _____

The Prayer Effect

Prayer was done with 20 cancer patients on chemotherapy, and who experienced anxiety, which brings on increased blood pressure, heart rate and high respiratory rate.

- Prayer was considered to be a complementary ___**v**__ for cancer treatment, causing a positive effect.
- Through prayer, the _____**w**___ of participants' anxiety was reduced greatly from moderate to mild levels.

Carvalho, C. C., Chaves, E. de C. L., Lunes, D. H., Simão, T. P., Grasselli, C. Da S. M., Braga, C. G. (2014). Effectiveness of prayer in reducing anxiety in cancer patients. *Journal of School of Nursing*, 48 (4), 684-690.

23.

v. _____

w. _____

Divine Prescription

Individuals are encouraged to keep their thoughts free from being troubled with cares of life by presenting your concerns to Christ, the Healing Redeemer and Provider. Emotionally, we are advised to cease from accommodating negative emotions such as anger, envy and rage and display human virtues such as kindness, patience and tolerance. The foundational perspective is captured in the biblical text: Be careful, or your hearts will be weighed down with carousing, drunkenness and the anxieties of life, and that day will close on you suddenly like a trap.

Mt 6:25-34; Lk 21:34.

24.

Absorb Fresh Air and Sunlight

In a study of 783 Finnish employees, whose average age was 47 years, researchers investigated the profile of workers who were exposed to nature and its relationship to occupational well-being. About 68% of participants had a high-profile exposure to nature, contributing to favourable, _____x_____ well-being.

The participants reported higher work engagement in terms of vigour and dedication than did the participants in the low exposure profile.

Hyvönen, K., Törnroos, K., Salonen, K., Korpela, K., Feldt, T., Kinnunen, U. (2018). Profiles of Nature Exposure and Outdoor Activities Associated with Occupational Well-Being Among Employees. *Frontiers in Psychology*, 9 (754).

25.

x. _____

Inhale Nature

Life in the open air is good for body and mind. It is God's medicine for the _____y_____ of health. Pure air, good water, sunshine, the beautiful surroundings of nature—these are His means for restoring the sick to health in natural ways. To the sick it is worth more than silver or gold to lie in the sunshine or in the shade of the trees.

White, E. G. (1923). *Counsels on Health* (Mountain View, CA: Pacific Press Publishing Association, p.166.

26.

y. _____

Summary

> ➤ Non-modifiable factors such as family history and modifiable factors such as unforgiveness and coping strategies contribute to an individual's emotional ill-health.

> ➤ The eight (8) **HEALINGS** health principles are inter-related and should be followed in order for there to be a positive impact on your emotional health.

> ➤ You can improve your emotional health by improving your lifestyle.

Insightful Perspectives

> **a)** Turn to **pages 24-25** in *Set the Captives Free Manual (Resource Guide)*, and read the sub-section entitled 'Physical Healing'.
>
> **b)** Remember to read Chapter 3 'The Views of a Few' in *Raising the Wounded: Grasping for Hope in the Midst of Despair*.

Emotional Healthy Lifestyle Matters

Let's turn to the *emotional healthy lifestyle matters* section. These are activities and tasks we can engage in to aid our emotional, physical, psychological, relational, social and spiritual development. Some of these can be done on your own at home.

TASKS TO AID WITH HEALING EMOTIONAL WOUNDS

The human nervous system consists of various neurotransmitters such as dopamine, oxytocin and serotonin. A popular function of serotonin, the body's natural anti-depressant, is to help regulate metabolism, appetite and mood. The body naturally produces serotonin, however, the brain only produces 2% of the body's total serotonin. This can be boosted by eating foods that are rich in protein amino acids. A large number of the body's serotonin is used by blood vessels and muscles. Foods that improve your mood during winter, aid the process that involves the tryptophan enzyme in association with oxygen and iron. The consumption of foods rich in carbohydrates, tryptophan and amino acids assist with the increase the body's insulin production. The insulin helps transport branch-chained amino acids to muscle cells, thereby allowing more tryptophan to get to the brain. As soon as tryptophan reaches the brain, it is then converted to serotonin.

External factors can also stimulate serotonin production in the brain. One way by which this occurs is through the quality of sleep an individual gets, since this can affect the production of serotonin. The "circadian rhythm" occurs when the SCN (Super-achiasmatic Nucleus) of the hypothalamus, which regulates the natural clock of the body, awakens the body to when it is night and when it is day.

1. Sleep Detox

TASK 1:

Every hour of sleep we get before **12 MIDNIGHT** is worth 2 hours of sleep after midnight. **Follow the guidelines below for every night of this new week.** In order to aid the body in managing stress, regulating brain function and afford serotonin to be converted into melatonin, you need at least 7 hours of sleep. Evaluate yourself with the chart below each morning, using the scale. Circle the appropriate letter (A, B or C) to indicate YOUR PROGRESS.

A I have **adjusted my schedule** for bed-time and waking time and **habitually followed** the guidelines to get a good quality of sleep.

B I have **partly followed** the guidelines to get a good quality of sleep.

C So far I have **not followed** the guidelines for adequate sleep.

Activity	*Scale*		
1. Set yourself not to consume any food or water after 7: 00 pm.	**A**	**B**	**C**
2. Adjust and maintain a regular schedule for bed- and waking -time			
3. Sleep in a clean, comfortable, dark and quiet room.			
4. Leave a window open where possible.			
5. Set aside arguments and worries and clear your conscience.			
6. Engage in moderate to vigorous daily physical activity.			
7. Ensure that your medication does not interfere with your sleep.			

VICTOR MARSHALL

2. Set the Mood

Put on a DVD with classical/ instrumental music for about five (5) minutes. Afterwards, turn the music off. This seeks to create a quiet and peaceful atmosphere for you to engage in this week's tasks.

3. Maintain Your Physical Activity Programme

Most lifestyle changes need time to make an impact, so that you can benefit from the changes. This section seeks to encourage you to stick with your exercise routine consistently and you will *see improvement.*

a. How consistent are you exercising/engage in physical activity for 30 minutes or more per day for at least five days a week?
   YES   **NO**   **NOT YET**

b. If *yes,* keep up the good work and do not let anything disrupt your routine not your healthy practice.

c. If no, or not yet, think about what may be hindering you from accomplishing your goal. **Review** the possible choices in SESSION ONE's Lifestyle Matters on **Page 13** in this *Companion Folder.* **SELECT** at least one you will do this week.

d. Write it here_____

4. Goal-setting

Setting realistic goals is a feature of developing optimism which is linked to **hope**, the first component of the **HEALINGS** health principles During this week, think of the realistic personal achievements (e.g: purchase a much-needed item, start a physical exercise routine etc) you desire to accomplish.

TASK 1:

My Realistic Goal I desire to accomplish this week/month is as follows:

_____

_____

_____

_____

_____

TASK 2:

Identify the steps which could aid you in achieving your goal for this week/month.

STEP 1:

_____

_____

_____

_____

STEP 2:

_____

_____

_____

_____

STEP 3:

_____

_____

_____

_____

OTHER STEPS:

_____

_____

_____

_____

_____

_____

_____

_____

_____

_____

_____

5. Assessment

Turn to the Assessment and Evaluation Tools Kit and complete the **Physical Self-care and Wellness Assessment** relating to your physical wellness. As you work through the statements, seek to be as honest as possible and be very demanding on yourself.

Personal Reflection (WEEK 3)

- What have you learnt about yourself so far in the programme?

....

....

....

....

- What specific aspect of yourself needs adjusting, improving or transforming?

....

....

....

....

- Write down **ONE (1)** idea/activity you learnt about in Session 3 and that you are planning to put into practice in your personal life. (**E.g** listening to instrumental music). **Why did you choose this activity?**

....

....

....

....

- How do you think this activity can help you address your emotional difficulties?

....

....

....

....

Emotional Health Lifestyle Scorecard

Week _____

ACTIVITY	DAY OF THE WEEK AND DATE						
	Sun ----/----/----	Mon ----/----/----	Tues ----/----/----	Wed ----/----/----	Thurs ----/----/----	Fri ----/----/----	Sat ----/----/----
Spiritual Engagement * Prepare for the journey of restoration with spiritual practices (See *Set the Captives Free Workbook*, pp.15, 73)							
Relationship Building Pray for a particular family member/relative/friend with whom you are having difficulty							
Exercise Engage in Exercise. State the type and amount of time daily							
Goal-setting Identify two or three things you wish to accomplish daily AND MONTHLY. This inspires hope and optimism in that you would have accomplished a goal							
Discussion Time * Identify any two (2) issues to be addressed with a particular family member/relative/friend, and prayerfully talk to that person about the issues							
Personal Reflection How much time have you spent on the reflection activity at the end of each SESSION?							
Special Reading On a daily basis, read ten (10) verses from the Gospel of St Mark 1-12. Also identify and MEMORISE the verse that attracts you.	*Verses Read*	*Verses Read*	*Verses Read*	*Verses Read*	*Verses Read*	*Verses Read*	*Verses Read*
.... *Favourite Verse(s)*	....						....
Water How many glasses of water did you drink during the day?							

NOTE: * Place a tick (√) in the box next to these items to show that you have completed the activity on a daily basis. It is expected that these activities will take time and will be on-going.

NOTES

Feel free to use this space to write out the verse you are memorising from the chapter you have read this week, as a way of helping you internalise the text.

Session Four

Foods to Boost Your Mood

During this session, pay attention to:

1) The relationship between food addiction and mental well-being.

2) Nutritional content of addictive foods.

3) The relationship between chronic diseases and emotional health.

4) Foods that can improve your well-being.

You will notice in your workbook that you have the outline of the PowerPoint presentation for **Session Four**, so that you may follow along.

DVD/PowerPoint Slides

Session Four

Foods to Boost Your Mood

During the PowerPoint presentations, feel free to follow along with the slides that correspond with those in the session. You can fill in the blank spaces with the missing words. Use the blanks in the margin with the letters that match to the letters on the blanks in the PowerPoint slides. (For example, for blank [z], write the answer on the line next to the section of the slide marked [z].

1.

> # EMOTIONAL HEALTH RESTORATION PROGRAMME
>
> Identifying Emotional Dys-functionality and Possible Solutions

2.

> ## Session 4
>
> ## Foods to Boost Your Mood

The Twelve 'Risk' Categories

1. Emotional Instability
2. Emotional Hurt
3. Lifestyle
4. **Nutrition**
5. Forgiveness
6. Abuse
7. Unresolved Issues
8. Inability to Cope
9. Medical Condition
10. Childhood Adversity
11. Psychological Needs
12. Mental Functioning

3.

Food Addiction and Mental Wellbeing

Food addiction has been linked to issues relating to comorbid mental health concerns and specific personality dimensions in relation to heightened motivations for substance use. For example, people with high anxiety sensitivity tend to engage in misuse of alcohol to reduce anxiety. Individuals who have a high level of hopelessness are more likely to experience major depressive episodes, thereby leading to alcohol consumption in order to relieve negative moods.

Source: Burrows, T., Hides, L., Brown, R., Dayas, C.V., & Kay-Lambkin, F. (2017). Differences in Dietary Preferences, Personality and Mental Health in Australian Adults with and without Food Addiction. *Nutrients*, 9(3):285.

4.

Food Processing and Addiction

Highly processed foods tend to be consumed in an addictive behaviour. This occurs because processing original foods into another substance may increase that substance's addictive potential. For example, processing grapes into wine, results in elevating the dose, or concentration, of the addictive agent (e.g: alcohol, and sugar) and speed up its rate of absorption into the bloodstream. This is indicative that refined carbohydrates (e.g., sugar, white flour) and fat are principal contributors to addictive-like eating.

Schulte, E. M., Avena, N. M. and, Gearhardt, A. N. (2015). Which Foods May Be Addictive? The Roles of Processing, Fat Content, and Glycemic Load. PLoS ONE 10(2).

5.

6.

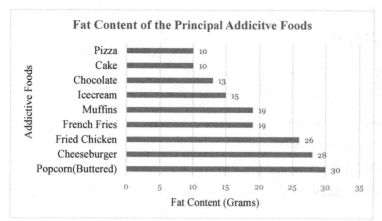

7.

a. _____

Effect of Addictive Foods

Foods such as cheeseburger, French Fries, and buttered popcorn are high in fat and refined products, be it white flour or sugar. They negatively affect us in terms of the ___**a**___ at which glucose enter the bloodstream, the amount of glucose per serving of the foods and how high our blood sugar could reach after eating these foods.

8.

Effect of Addictive Foods

The consumption of high-fat, high-sugar foods, added fat and/or refined carbohydrates such as white flour or sugar (e.g., pizza, chocolate, chips) may uniquely activate the reward system in a manner similar to drug misuse, thereby, triggering compulsive eating behaviour.

Burrows, T., Hides, L., Brown, R., Dayas, C.V., & Kay-Lambkin, F. (2017). Differences in Dietary Preferences, Personality and Mental Health in Australian Adults with and without Food Addiction. *Nutrients*, 9(3):285.

9.

Chronic Disease and Wellbeing

Atherosclerosis or the hardening and build-up of plaque in the arteries is the main explanation for the beginning of Cardio-vascular disease and for the connection between mental illness and Cardio-vascular diseases. Depression is seen as a catalyst of coronary atherosclerosis because of the associated reduction in neuro-transmitters (e.g., serotonin) that, in turn, have been shown to affect the shape and aggregation reactivity of platelets. Depression as a psychological disorder contributes to the build-up of coronary plaques.

10.

b. _____

Chronic Disease and Wellbeing

The prevalence of any cardio-vascular disease is highest among adults who have the worst profile of ____**b**____ health, in terms of having major depression and languishing in life.

Keyes, C. L. M. (2004). The nexus of cardiovascular disease and depression revisited: the complete mental health perspective and the moderating role of age and gender. *Aging & Mental Health*, 8(3): 266–274 (272).

11.

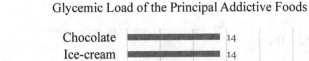

Glycemic Load of the Principal Addictive Foods

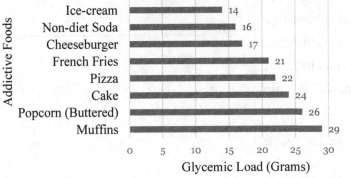

Addictive Food	Glycemic Load (Grams)
Chocolate	14
Ice-cream	14
Non-diet Soda	16
Cheeseburger	17
French Fries	21
Pizza	22
Cake	24
Popcorn (Buttered)	26
Muffins	29

Gender and Food Addiction

A total of 1344 individuals were recruited to investigate food addiction and how it is associated with dietary intake, personality traits and mental health issues. Females were more likely to have food addiction than males, and three times at risk of _____**c**_____ food addiction. Individuals who consume less healthy foods including sweetened drinks, and confectionary (chocolates and lollies) were diagnosed with food addiction.

Burrows, T., Hides, L., Brown, R., Dayas, C.V., & Kay-Lambkin, F. (2017). Differences in Dietary Preferences, Personality and Mental Health in Australian Adults with and without Food Addiction. *Nutrients*, 9(3):285.

12.

c. _____

Impact of foods on the Brain

Almost 100 years ago, counsel has been given about the negative impact of over-indulgence. Insightful counsel states that "some do not exercise control over their appetites, but indulge taste at the expense of _____**d**_____. As a result, the brain is clouded, their thoughts are sluggish, and they fail to accomplish what they might if they were self-denying and abstemious.

White, E. G. (1923). *Counsels on Health* (Mountain View, CA: Pacific Press Publishing Association, p.71

13.

d. _____

Nutritious Food for the Brain

The brain is the organ and instrument of the mind, and controls the whole body. In order for the other parts of the system to be healthy, the brain must be _____**e**_____. And in order for the brain to be healthy, the _____**f**_____ must be pure. If by correct habits of eating and drinking the blood is kept pure, the brain will be properly nourished

White, E. G. (1932). *Medical Ministry* (Boise, ID: Pacific Press Publishing Association), p.291.

14.

e. _____

f. _____

Diet and Food Addiction

A study of 462 participants, age 18-35 revealed that higher intakes of energy-dense and nutrient-poor foods including candy and take-out foods were associated with food addiction. These foods contain large quantities of added fat, sugar and salt (sodium) to increase their ____g____; hence, the positive relationship between dietary intakes of saturated fat, and food addiction.

Pursey, K. M., Collins, C. E., Stanwell, P., Burrows, T. L. (2015). Foods and dietary profiles associated with 'food addiction' in young adults. *Addictive Behaviors Reports*, 2, 41- 48 (46).

15.

g. _____

Impact of Chronic Disease on Emotional Health

Individuals with diabetes endeavour to self-manage their diet, medication and other aspects of self-care, while coping with demands of life. A ____h____ to achieving optimal control over their self-care is poor emotional wellbeing, thereby contributing to diabetes distress. For example, loss of interest in previously enjoyable activities, social withdrawal, along with disturbed sleep. Such individuals tend to be stuck in recurring thinking patterns that focus on failures and worthlessness.

Keen, A. J. A. (2019). The nature and impact of poor emotional wellbeing in people with diabetes. *Practical Diabetes*, 36 (4), 132–135 (132).

16.

h. _____

Blood Glucose Levels

Healthy non-diabetics usually have a ____i____ blood glucose level in the range of 4.0 to 5.4 mmol/L (UK) or 72 to 99 mg/dL (USA) when ____j____ or at the time of waking up from their night's sleep. It rises up to 7.8 mmol/L (140 mg/dL) 2 hours after eating a meal. The level should be 4 to 7 mmol/L for people with type 1 or type 2 diabetes before a meal, under 9 mmol/L for people with type 1 diabetes and under 8.5mmol/L for people with type 2 diabetes after a meal.

17.

i. _____

j. _____

Impact of Diet on Diabetes I

Types I and II diabetics can be aided in normalizing their blood sugar levels by an intake of foods very low in _____k_____, that is less than 3grams. Fresh citrus fruits such as apples, bananas, cherries and oranges provide anti-oxidants such as vitamin C which builds immunity. Other food groups low in fat are seeds and vegetable oils which produce vitamin E, another anti-oxidant needed for the functioning of organs such as the skin and the brain.

18.

k. _____

Impact of Diet on Diabetes II

Green leafy vegetables (e.g: lettuce, and spinach and other vegetables such as carrots and pumpkin are beneficial to our emotional and physical health. _____l_____ foods such as legumes (e.g: beans and peas) and wholewheat and whole grain foods (e.g: barley, brown rice) can bring about the essential _____m_____ impact of reducing the blood glucose level.

19.

l. _____

m. _____

Impact of Diet on Diabetes III

Carbohydrates consist of three major components namely starch and fibre, which are _____n_____ carbohydrates *and* sugar, a simple carbohydrate. It is recommended to use complex carbohydrate foods, or as they are grown. They consist of more _____o_____ compared to simple carbohydrates, since they contain more fibre, digest slowly, and they are more filling, thus, a better option to control weight. Fibre is also essential since it promotes regularity in the bowel and controls cholesterol.

20.

n. _____

o. _____

Impact of Chronic Disease on Emotional Health – Obesity

A psychological issue relating to obesity is body image dissatisfaction, in that a negative body image can have _____p_____ psychological consequences in obese people, including depressive symptoms and decreased _____q_____. For example, in a study of 142 obese individuals, those who over-valuated their shape was linked to having greater levels of eating-disorder psychopathology and poorer psychological functioning (e.g: higher depression and lower self-esteem levels).

Grilo, C. M., White, M. A., and Masheb, R. M. (2012). Significance of overvaluation of shape and weight in an ethnically diverse sample of obese patients with binge-eating disorder in primary care settings. *Behaviour Research and Therapy*, 50 (5), 298-303.

Positive _____r___ Promotes Physical Health

God is the great caretaker of the human machinery. In the care of our bodies, we must _____s_____ with Him. Love for God is essential for life and health.... In order to have perfect health our hearts must be filled with [positive emotions] love and hope and joy.

White, E. G. (1932). *Medical Ministry* (Boise, ID: Pacific Press Publishing Association), p.291.

Ancient Instructions

Since we are created in the image of the Divine Creator, we are expected to maintain the Divine input by being _____t_____ of how we treat our bodies. We are brought into account and reminded of our responsibility, through the question: Don't you realize that your body is the temple of the Holy Spirit, who lives in you and was given to you by God? You do not belong to yourself, **20** for [*The Divine Healer*] bought you with a high price. So you must honor God with your body (1 Cor 6:19-20, NLT).

21.

p. _____

q. _____

22.

r. _____

s. _____

23.

t. _____

Facts About Obesity

Body Mass Index (BMI) can be normal weight (18.6 - 24.9 kg/m2), overweight (25 - 29.9 kg/m2), clinical obesity (30 – 39.9 kg/m2), or severe/morbid obesity (40 kg/m2) or more than 35 kg/m2 in association with co-morbidities such as hypertension. Prevalence rates for overweight/obesity are between 28% - 35% in Caribbean countries. Data indicate that 60% of all deaths in the Region is due to non-communicable diseases (NCDs).

Henry, F. J. (2016). Obesity in the Caribbean: A Case for Public Policies. Journal of Nutritional Disorders and Therapy, 6 (3); Caribbean Public Health Agency. (2014). *Plan of Action for Promoting Healthy Weights in the Caribbean: Prevention and Control of Childhood Obesity 2014 – 2019* (Trinidad: CARPHA).

24.

Diet and _____u___

A study, examining stress and dietary behaviour in 407 Kuwaiti undergraduate students, of which 60% were females and 43% were stressed, found that the stressed females ate more of the _____v_____ energy-dense foods such as fast foods, snacks and beverages than the unstressed females. However, stressed males engaged in unhealthy dietary behaviour, in terms of consuming greater amounts of fast food.

Ahmed F, Al-Radhwan L, Al-Azmi GZS, Al-Beajan M (2014) Association between Stress and Dietary Behaviours among Undergraduate Students in Kuwait: Gender Differences. Journal of Nutrition and Health Science, 1(1).

25.

u. _____

v. _____

Diet and Affective disorder

The burden of chronic and non-communicable diseases bring about psychological _____w_____, displayed through negative emotions and feelings, and stress. Iron, magnesium and zinc _____x_____ contribute to anxiety and depression. Fibre-rich whole grains, nuts, seeds, greens, and legumes are beneficial seeing they are rich in _____y_____ and fibre. They also contain tryptophan, which is converted to serotonin, and provide healthy energy while reducing _____z_____.

Młyniec, K., Davies, C. L., Irene Go'mez de Aguero Sanchez, I. G. de A., Pytka, K., Bogusława Budziszewska, B. and Nowak, G. (2014). Essential elements in depression and anxiety. Part I. *Pharmacological Reports*, 66 (4), 534-544.

26.

w. _____

x. _____

y. _____

z. _____

Summary

➢ Highly processed foods negatively affect blood sugar levels.

➢ Chronic diseases such as diabetes bring on psychological distress in various forms, be it anxiety or depression.

➢ A very low fat and high-fibre diet can help reduce blood glucose levels.

➢ Various mineral deficiencies such as lack of iron and zinc can contribute to anxiety and depression.

Insightful Perspectives

a) Continue reading **pages 24-25** in *Set the Captives Free (Resource Guide)*, entitled 'Physical Healing

b) Remember to read *Chapter 4 in Raising the Wounded.*

Emotional Healthy Lifestyle Matters

Let's turn to the *emotional healthy lifestyle matters* section. These are activities and tasks we can engage in to aid our emotional, physical, psychological, relational, social and spiritual development. Some of these can be done on your own at home.

TASKS TO AID WITH EMOTIONAL AND SPIRITUAL WELLBEING

1. Practise Theological Reflection

This spiritual discipline requires that individuals acquire spiritual Guidance as they seek to trust in the Divine Creator and the Healing Messiah. This component of the HEALINGS health principles indicates that there is an inherent and vital relationship between one's spirituality and the healing process on various levels such as emotional, physical and psychological.

TASK 1:

a) Select **ONE** of the following texts, and pray through (or about)/reflect /meditate on the verses:

> O God, listen to my cry!
>
> > Hear my prayer!
>
> [2] From the ends of the earth,
>
> > I cry to you for help
> >
> > when my heart is overwhelmed.
>
> Lead me to the towering rock of safety,
>
> [3] for you are my safe refuge,
>
> > a fortress where my enemies cannot reach me.
>
> _____ **(Psalm 61:1-3, NLT)**

> I lie awake thinking of you,
>
> > meditating on you through the night.
>
> [7] Because you are my helper,
>
> > I sing for joy in the shadow of your wings.
>
> [8] I cling to you;
>
> > your strong right hand holds me securely.
>
> _____ **(Psalm 63:6-8, NLT)**

TASK 2:

On **pages 29-34,** In your *Set the Captives free: 12 Studies for Individuals or Groups* Workbook, you will find activities to assist you in examining different types of life cycles. Work through the activities on these pages as you seek to gauge where you are on the three types of life cycles.

VICTOR MARSHALL

2. Selecting Moody Foods

We have learnt that food can provide essential macro- (proteins) and micro-nutrients (iron, magnesium) that our brain and the body require. This week, seek to consume adequate portions of each food type on a daily basis, so that you can be supplied with tryptophan, vitamins, and minerals such as iron, magnesium and zinc. This also helps you address your Body Mass Index (BMI).

TASK 1:

1. Calculate your BMI, using the online calculator or manually. Insert you weight in kg or pounds and your height in metres (m) or feet (ft). My **BMI is** _____ kg/m^2.

2. Based on my BMI, my weight category is_____.

TASK 2:

1. I intend to reduce my fat intake by consuming less

   _____

   _____

   _____

   _____

2. In order to get adequate amount of iron, magnesium and zinc, I will consume the following:

   _____

   _____

   _____

   _____

3. I endeavour to consume the following foods so that I can have a high-fibre diet:

   _____

   _____

   _____

3. Monitoring Emotional Eating

TASK 1:

Examine the list of emotions in the chart and **circle** the ones you tend to experience most on a given day or in a given week.

Discouraged	Lonely	Scared	Humiliated	Irritated
Worried	Anxious	Relaxed	Accepted	Frustrated
Jealous	Sad	Tired	Bored	Confused
Happy	Nervous	Depressed	Hopeless	Unappreciated
Unloved	Afraid	Restless	Energetic	Peaceful
Excited	Confident	Angry	Helpless	Humiliated

TASK 2:

In the chart below, list some of the emotions you have circled. Beside each one, identify what food(s) you tend to eat when you are experiencing those emotions. Then identify non-food choices/activities which can provide a similar sensation as the foods you tend to use.

Emotions Experienced	Food(s) Associated with these Emotions	Healthy Non-food Optional Action(s)
Example: Unappreciated	*Ice-cream, chocolate*	*Reading a book; listening to classical/Gospel/favourite song*

4. Therapeutic Evaluation

The task requires you to examine another aspect of your psychological well-being. Review the stress questionnaires and anxiety questionnaires and complete the following data: **(a)** stress load _____ **(b)** stress level _____ and **(c)** anxiety level _____.

If you are beyond **'mild'** on your stress and anxiety scores, plan to add another type of physical activity to your exercise programme. Additionally, review and complete **Task 1** on **Page 41** and Numbers 2 and 3 on **Page 59**. Afterwards, work through **Task 1** using the *OTHER* biblical text on **Page 76**.

5. Review from Previous Sessions

In the previous weeks, you have taken into account various emotional healthy lifestyle matters, all relating to emotional wounded-ness. These areas are listed below. Please circle the answer for each activity to indicate whether or not you have been taking part in these activities. The superscript number indicates the session where each lifestyle matter is found.

Flush the mind through wholesome activities[1]	Doing	Not Doing
Consistent Exercise Activities[1,3]	Doing	Not Doing
Learn about and practice self-awareness[1,2,]	Doing	Not Doing
Adequate water intake[2]	Doing	Not Doing
Engage in spiritual disciplines (Devotions)[1,2,3]	Doing	Not Doing
Identify your degree of emotional wounded-ness[3]	Doing	Not Doing
Identify your emotional type/style of relating[1]	Doing	Not Doing
Engage in spiritual disciplines (Intercessory Prayer)[1,2,3]	Doing	Not Doing
Replace negative thoughts with inspired material[2]	Doing	Not Doing
Practise spiritual activities[3] (Reading sacred material)	Doing	Not Doing
Implement goals for physical and spiritual wellbeing[2,3]	Doing	Not Doing
Engage in sleep detox[3]	Doing	Not Doing
Practise Goal-setting[3]	Doing	Not Doing
Implementing goals for physical and spiritual self-care[2,3]	Doing	Not Doing

Plans & Goal Setting

On the lines below, write out **a plan for each Lifestyle activity** you need to adopt /start to practise from the list above. State the possible day/date that you will seek to incorporate your new habits. Also review the suggestions in the appropriate previous sessions, as stated in this *Companion Folder.*

....

....

....

....

....

....

....

....

....

....

....

....

....

....

....

....

....

....

....

....

....

VICTOR MARSHALL

Personal Reflective Study Session (WEEK 4)

Prayerfully review the biblical text below:

"Don't you realize that your body is the temple of the Holy Spirit, who lives in you and was given to you by God? You do not belong to yourself, [20] for God bought you with a high price. So you must honor God with your body."
(1 Corinthians 6:19-20, NLT).

- What impact did this session have on you?

....

....

....

....

....

- Write out an insight that you have gained from the above-mentioned Sacred Writing.

....

....

....

....

....

- How important is it for you to follow the counsel in this Biblical text which instruct you to look after your physical body in a greater way? Share your thoughts below.

....

....

....

....

....

Emotional Health Lifestyle Scorecard

Week _____

ACTIVITY	DAY OF THE WEEK AND DATE						
	Sun ----/----/----	Mon ----/----/----	Tues ----/----/----	Wed ----/----/----	Thurs ----/----/----	Fri ----/----/----	Sat ----/----/----
Spiritual Engagement * Prepare for the journey of restoration with spiritual practices (See *Set the Captives Free Workbook*, pp.15, 73							
Relationship Building Pray for a particular family member/relative/friend with whom you are having difficulty							
Exercise Engage in Exercise. State the type and amount of time daily							
Goal-setting Identify two or three things you wish to accomplish daily AND MONTHLY. This inspires hope and optimism in that you would have accomplished a goal							
Discussion Time * Identify any two (2) issues to be addressed with a particular family member/relative/friend, and prayerfully talk to that person about the issues							
Personal Reflection How much time have you spent on the reflection activity at the end of each **SESSION?**							
Special Reading On a daily basis, read ten (10) verses from the Gospel of St Mark 1-12. Also identify and **MEMORISE** the verse that attracts you.	*Verses Read*	*Verses Read*	*Verses Read*	*Verses Read*	*Verses Read*	*Verses Read*	*Verses Read* ....
Favourite Verse(s)							
Water How many glasses of water did you drink during the day?							

NOTE: * Place a tick (√) in the box next to these items to show that you have completed the activity on a daily basis. It is expected that these activities will take time and will be on-going.

NOTES

Feel free to use this space to write out the verse you are memorising from the chapter you have read this week, as a way of helping you internalise the text.

Session Five
Forgiveness: Its Healing Power (Part 1)

During this session, pay attention to:

1) The first two stages in the journey towards forgiveness.

2) Spiritual and psychological resources needed to promote emotional wellness

3) Skills such as reframing

4) The importance of qualities such as compassion, empathy and 'safe vulnerability'.

5) Physiological reactions due to a display and an internalization of negative emotions.

You will notice in your workbook that you have the outline of the PowerPoint presentation for **Session Five**, so that you may follow along.

DVD/PowerPoint Slides

Session Five

Forgiveness: Its Healing Power (Part 1)

During the PowerPoint presentations, feel free to follow along with the slides that correspond with those in the session. You can fill in the blank spaces with the missing words. Use the blanks in the margin with the letters that match to the letters on the blanks in the PowerPoint slides. (For example, for blank [a], write the answer on the line next to the section of the slide marked [a].)

1.

> ## EMOTIONAL HEALTH RESTORATION PROGRAMME
>
> Identifying Emotional Dys-functionality and Possible Solutions

2.

> ## Session 5
>
> Forgiveness: Its Healing Power
> (Part I)

3.

The Twelve 'Risk' Categories

1. Emotional Instability
2. Emotional Hurt
3. Lifestyle
4. Nutrition
5. **Unforgiveness**
6. Abuse
7. Unresolved Issues
8. Inability to Cope
9. Medical Condition
10. Childhood Adversity
11. Psychological Needs
12. Mental Functioning

4.

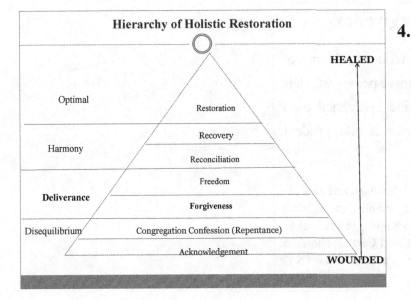

Hierarchy of Holistic Restoration

HEALED

Optimal — Restoration

Harmony — Recovery / Reconciliation

Deliverance — Freedom / **Forgiveness**

Disequilibrium — Congregation Confession (Repentance) / Acknowledgement

WOUNDED

5.

Biblical Perspective of Forgiveness

Forgiveness, as a spiritual practice, is essential for achieving reconciliation. This religious practice is biblically grounded, in that we are advised that "if you forgive those who sin against you, your heavenly Father will forgive you. But if you refuse to forgive others, your Father will not forgive your sins.

Mt 6: 14-15, NLT

Definitions of Forgiveness

"Forgiveness involves the process of ___a_____ one's anger and hurt from the past, with the goal of _____b_____ one's peace in the present and revitalizing one's purpose and hopes for the future."

(Dick Tibbitts, *Forgive To Live: How Forgiveness Can Save Your Life* (Nashville, TN: Thomas Nelson, 2006,) p.5

Definitions of Forgiveness

Forgiveness is "a motivation to reduce avoidance of and retaliation (or revenge) against a person who has harmed or offended one, and to increase conciliation between the parties if conciliation is safe, prudent and possible."

(Everett L. Worthington, Jr, Steven J. Sandage and Jack W. Berry, "Group Interventions to Promote Forgiveness: What Researchers and Clinicians Ought to Know" in Michael E. McCullough, Kenneth I. Pargament, and Carl E. Thoresen (eds), *Forgiveness: Theory, Research, and Practice* (NY: Guilford Press, 2001), p. 229.

Levels of Forgiveness

Forgiveness occurs on three levels namely: horizontal/interpersonal/relational, _____c_____, _____d_____, _____e_____ and personal/intra-personal. However, the focus of this programme is on horizontal forgiveness, which implies extending forgiveness to and receiving it from another person or the Divine One.

6.

a. _____

b. _____

7.

8.

c. _____

d. _____

e. _____

Impact of Un-forgiveness

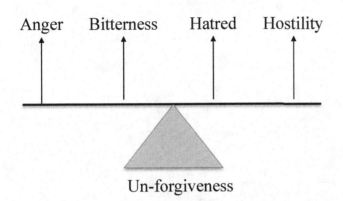

Anger   Bitterness   Hatred   Hostility

Un-forgiveness

9.

Un-forgiveness is a major

f. _____

component in the display of
higher order (tertiary)

g. _____

10.

h. _____

Physiological Impact of Unforgiveness

A review of empirical studies revealed that unforgiveness may be dominated by emotions such as bitterness, fear or _____h_____. Depending on which one dominates, different physiological processes are likely to emerge as are different health outcomes. For example, anger, especially hostile, and seething anger, particularly affects the heart.

Everett L. Worthington and Goli Sotooh. (2010). Physiological Assessment of Forgiveness, Grudges, and Revenge: Theories, Research Methods, and Implications. *International Journal of Psychology Research,* 5, (3/4), 291-316 (296).

Stage One

In order to embark on this journey towards forgiveness, it is essential to have a willingness to ___i___ and display various qualities. Also it is vital to ___j___ and maintain our own emotional _____k_____.
Thus, we need at least two types of resources to aid us in _____l_____ our emotional wellness: spiritual and _____m____ resources.

Marshall, *On the Road to Forgiveness*, p.3

11.

i. _____

j. _____

k. _____

l. _____

m. _____

Healing Power of Forgiveness

12.

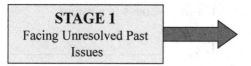

STAGE 1
Facing Unresolved Past
Issues

Spiritual Resources: Prayer

13.

A study among American war veterans indicates that praying for assistance with personal issues was associated with less posttraumatic stress disorder symptoms, and praying frequently for calmness and to be focused also resulted in lower depression.

Rhondie Tait, Joseph M. Currier & J. Irene Harris. (2015). Prayer Coping, Disclosure of Trauma, and Mental Health Symptoms among Recently Deployed United States Veterans of the Iraq and Afghanistan Conflicts. *The International Journal for the Psychology of Religion,* 26(1), 1-15.

Spiritual Resources: Theological Reflection

14.

n. _____

This is a method by which people learn from and use their own experience, _____ **n** _____ and action, whereby a person (or group) is helped to discover God's presence in that person's (or group's) individual experience."

Robert L. Kinast, *Let Ministry Teach: A Guide to Theological Reflection* (Collegeville, MN: Liturgical Press, 1996), pp. viii, x.

Theological Reflection

Theological reflection uses resources such as corporate and personal forms of _____o_____, Sacred Scripture, and prayer for reflection and _____p_____ _____q_____ of events. Meanwhile, its primary goal is to help individuals recognise and respond to the Divine presence as it blends _____r_____ with theology.

Kinast, *Let Ministry Teach*, p. xiv

15.

o. _____

p. _____

q. _____

r. _____

The Reframing Process

It is also important that we ___s___ our difficult circumstances. This means examining the situation through another lens/ or from a different ___t___. In order to reframe an event, a person is encouraged to have a different ___u___ of the issue so that the meaning or impact is seen from a different angle/ perspective. This produces a different __v___, allowing individuals to see their problem in a more favourable light.

16.

s. _____

t. _____

u. _____

v. _____

The Reframing Process

It is also important that we ___w___ our difficult circumstances. This means examining the situation through another lens/ or from a different ___x___. In order to reframe an event, a person is encouraged to have a different ___y___ of the issue so that the meaning or impact is seen from a different angle/ perspective. This produces a different __z___, allowing individuals to see their problem in a more favourable light.

17.

w. _____

x. _____

y. _____

z. _____

Therapeutic Resources: Psychotherapy

A study, occurred with 137 participants. 68 received therapeutic treatment, were in the control group. The psychotherapy aided patients in extending:

_____**a2**_____.

They also expressed more _____**b2**_____, greater _____**c2**_____, and less _____**d2**_____.

Mróz, J., Kaleta, K. (2020). Forgiveness and Mental Health Variables among Psychotherapy Outpatients. Annales Universitatis Mariae Curie-Skłodowska. Sectio J, Paedagogia-Psychologia, 33(3), 145-159.

18.

a2._____

b2._____

c2._____

d2._____

Biblical Foundation

Forgiveness is a reciprocal response to a transgression which was experienced within an interpersonal context. In light of this view, Christ, the All-powerful, Healing Messiah reinforces the foundation for our healing, be it on the emotional or spiritual level. The counsel indicates that we will not be freed from our debts/transgressions "If each of you, from his heart, does not forgive his brother his trespasses."

Matthew 18:35, NLT.

19.

Exhibition of Qualities

324 undergraduates, age 18-51, were studied to explore the relationship between empathy and forgiveness. It was predicted that individuals with a:

- High level of _____**e2**_____ usually have a high level of forgiveness towards others.

Ann Macaskill , John Malt by & Liza Day (2002) Forgiveness of Self and Others and Emotional Empathy, *The Journal of Social Psychology*, 142 (5),, 663-665 (664).

20.

e2._____

Specific Qualities

'Safe vulnerability' enables us to:

- _____f2_____ ourselves to moments of tears and pain. .

- ___g2___ the revengeful attitude.

- display honesty, _____h2_____ and a high measure of _____i2_____. They can assist you in monitoring your level of maturity.

Marshall, *On the Road to Forgiveness*, p.52.

21.

f2._____

g2._____

h2._____

i2._____

Healing Power of Forgiveness

STAGE 1	STAGE 2
Facing Unresolved Past Issues	Surrender the unresolved Past

22.

Insight

The relation that exists between the mind and the body is very intimate. When one is affected, the other sympathizes. The condition of the mind affects the health to a far greater degree than many realize. Many of the diseases from which men suffer are the result of mental depression. Effects of Negative Emotions: Grief, anxiety, discontent, remorse, guilt, distrust, all tend to break down the life forces and to invite decay and death.

White, *Ministry of Healing*, p.241.

23.

Negative Emotions and the Brain

Un-surrendered painful issues can bring out negative emotions and affect the brain. For example,

- A continuous bout of _____**j2**___ impairs the amygdala.

The pre-frontal cortex manages the amygdala by controlling our reaction to the anger.

- A ____**k2**_____ PFC affects how we regulate emotions such as anger.

24.

j2. _____

k2. _____

Impact of Negative Emotions

Research supports this biological perspective. Individuals who respond negatively to an _____**l2** _____event, with moods such as anxiety or feelings such as envy, tend to display physiological reactions such as high _____**m2** _____ and increase heart rate.

Allan, A., & McKillop, D. (2010). The health implications of apologizing after an adverse event, *International Journal for Quality in Health Care*, 22 (2), pp. 126–131 (127).

25.

l2. _____

m2. _____

Impact of un-surrendered Issues

Individuals who hold on to un-surrendered painful issues tend to

- experience _____**n2**_____ in various proportions

- employ one or more _____**o2**_____ _____.

- lose out on getting higher order psychological _____**p2**_____ being met.

Marshall, *On the Road to Forgiveness*, p.20.

26.

n2. _____

o2. _____

p2. _____

Impact of Negative Emotions

Anger, hatred and other negative emotions are often kept sealed on the inside. Such individuals tend to engage in unusual behaviours such as _____q2_____ their friends, and withdrawing from ____r2_____ gatherings, thus leading them to become _____s2_____ dysfunctional.

Marshall, *On the Road to Forgiveness*, p.23.

Biblical Perspective

A battle takes place in the mind, when we have unresolved issues. However, we can be helped if we take the counsel where we are reminded that God "will keep in perfect_____t2_____ those whose minds are steadfast, because they _____u2_____ in you.

Isaiah 26:3 (NIV).

Insight

"Those who would not fall a prey to Satan's devices must guard well the avenues of the soul; they must avoid reading, seeing, or hearing that which will suggest impure thoughts. The mind should not be left to wander at random upon every subject that the adversary of souls may suggest."

White, *Messages to Young People,* p.285

27.

q2._____

r2._____

s2._____

28.

t2. _____

u2._____

29.

Summary

> Spiritual resources such as intercessory prayer and theological reflection, along with therapeutic resources can assist us in promoting emotional wellness.

> Reframing is one way by which we can surrender emotionally- difficult issues.

> A number of personal qualities such as safe vulnerability are necessary in order to develop the capacity to surrender the past painful issues.

Insightful Perspectives

> **a)** Turn to the chapter entitled 'Five-Dimensional Perspective of Holistic Restoration in *Set the Captives Free (Resource Guide)* Manual and read the sub-section entitled 'Spiritual Revival/Renewal'.
>
> **b)** Remember to read Chapters 1 & 2 in the book: *On the Road to Forgiveness*, **Pages 1-32.**

Emotional Healthy Lifestyle Matters

Let's turn to the *emotional healthy lifestyle matters* section. These are activities and tasks we can engage in to aid our emotional, physical, psychological, relational, social and spiritual development. Some of these can be done on your own at home.

TASKS TO AID WITH EMOTIONAL AND SPIRITUAL WELLBEING

1. Practise Theological Reflection

This spiritual discipline requires that individuals acquire spiritual **G**uidance as they seek to trust in the Divine Creator and the Healing Messiah. This component of the HEALINGS health principles indicates that there is an inherent and vital relationship between one's spirituality and the healing process on various levels such as emotional, physical and psychological.

TASK 1:

(a) Select **ONE** of the following texts, read and pray through (or about)/reflect /meditate on the verses. Seek to memorize the verse which attracts your attention.

> Purify me from my sins,[c] and I will be clean;
>> wash me, and I will be whiter than snow.
>
> 8 Oh, give me back my joy again;
>> you have broken me—
>> now let me rejoice.
>
> 9 Don't keep looking at my sins.
>> Remove the stain of my guilt.
>
> 10 Create in me a clean heart, O God.
>> Renew a loyal spirit within me.
>
> 11 Do not banish me from your presence,
>> and don't take your Holy Spirit[d] from me.
>
> 12 Restore to me the joy of your salvation,
>> and make me willing to obey you.
>
> _____(Psalm 51:7-12, NLT).

(b) Read this text from the Ancient Sacred Word and complete the missing words:

> The LORD is my light and my salvation—
>> so why should I be afraid?
>
> The LORD is my fortress, _____ me from danger,
>> so why should I tremble?
>
> 2 When evil people come to devour me,
>> when my enemies and foes attack me,
>> they will stumble and fall.
>
> 3 Though a mighty army surrounds me,
>> my heart will not be _____.
>
> Even if I am attacked,
>> I will remain confident.
>
> _____ (Psalm 27:1-3, NLT).

(c) What insights or message did you gain from the text? To what extent is the Divine One involved in your personal issues?

....

....

....

....

2. Building Relationships

Healthy and positive **interpersonal relationships**, the fifth component of the HEALINGS health principles, require a display of wholesome attitudes and behaviours and healthy interactions with others. One way to achieve this is to engage emotionally by working through the material relating to the Journey Towards Forgiveness, which we will commence in this **Session**, and continue to explore in the next Session.

TASK 1:

a)In your *Set the Captives free: 12 Studies for Individuals or Groups* Workbook, on **pages 46–52**, you will find activities to assist you in taking the Journey Towards Forgiveness. Work through the activities on these pages as you seek to begin extending and receiving forgiveness.

3. Learn to Reframe Your Emotionally Difficult Experiences

TASK 1:

a)Read through Philippians 3:7-9.

"But what things were gain to me, these I have counted loss for Christ. [8] Yet indeed I also count all things loss for the excellence of the knowledge of Christ Jesus my Lord, for whom I have suffered the loss of all things, and count them as rubbish, that I may gain Christ [9] and be found in Him, not having my own righteousness, which *is* from the law, but that which *is* through faith in Christ, the righteousness which is from God by faith;"

Here is a useful quotation

> "A tender spirit, a gentle, winning deportment, may save the erring and hide a multitude of sins. The revelation of Christ in your own character will have a transforming power upon all with whom you come in contact." White, *Thoughts from the Mount of Blessings*, p. 129.

b)Can you identify with this new action? How can you look at the emotional difficulties in your life differently?

....

....

....

....

....

TASK 2:

a)Read prayerfully **Isaiah 43:18-19.** Review **Task 1** on **Page 37** in this ***Companion Folder*** and continue working on this task. Otherwise, reflect on how Isaiah 43:18-19 is helpful to you at this stage of your journey.

> "Do not remember the former things,
> Nor consider the things of old.
> ¹⁹ Behold, I will do a new thing,
> Now it shall spring forth;
> Shall you not know it?
> I will even make a road in the wilderness
> *And* rivers in the desert.
>
> _____ (Isaiah 43:18-19, NKJV).

4. Reprogramming the Brain

A continuous bout of anger raging through the amygdala and left unaddressed tends to create a new pathway/shortcut, which affects the regulation of emotions in the brain. In order to 'close off' this pathway and provide a normal channel, various techniques can be used. Plan to engage in these 3 activities to help address the anger so you can control and manage this emotion.

TASK 1:

In the event that a situation generates angry feelings in you, to the extent that your temper flares, it is a signal that you need to use relaxation skills.

a) Practise a few **deep-breathing exercises**, such as inhaling and exhaling briskly. Focus on a relaxing scene such as being at the beach or in the park, while you perform the short exercises.
b) Play and listen to music, even while you are engaged in the relaxing exercises.

TASK 2

In the midst of the moment or situation, take a **time out** by counting from 1 to 10 in order to get some quiet time so that you are better prepared to handle the situation without becoming irritated or angry.

(a)I will do this during my quiet moments:

_____

_____

_____

_____

_____

_____

_____

_____

TASK 3

(a) Fit the parts of the following text in the correct order by connecting them with an arrow.

i)	to be angry,	ii)	Do not be
iii)	eager in your heart	iv)	dwells in the heart of fools
v)	For anger		

_____ (Ecclesiastes 7:9, AMP).

(b) Write out the text in the space below as you internalize and recite it a few times a day.

_____

_____

_____

_____

_____

5. Assessment

Turn to the Assessment and Evaluation Tools Kit and take some time to complete the **Relational Self-care and Wellness Assessment,** relating to your relational health. While working through the statements, seek to be as honest as possible and be very demanding on yourself.

Personal Reflective Study Session (WEEK 5)

Prayerfully REVIEW the definitions of forgiveness on Page 88 in this *Companion Folder.*
See Also Page xxix in the Book, *On the Road to Forgiveness.*

- Which definition attracted your attention the most? Why?

....

....

....

....

....

....

....

....

....

....

- How important is it for you to forgive the person who has caused you pain (who has displayed undesirable attitudes and behaviours towards you)?

....

....

....

....

....

....

....

....

....

VICTOR MARSHALL

- What impact do you think it would have on you **AND** on the individual?

....
....
....
....
....
....
....
....
....
....
....
....

- How did the **first two stages** of the journey towards forgiveness help you emotionally, psychologically and (or) spiritually?

....
....
....
....
....
....
....
....
....
....
....
....

- How willing or ready are/ were you to go through the **first two stages** of the journey towards forgiveness? What difficulties will/did you face?

....
....
....
....
....
....
....
....
....
....
....
....
....
....
....
....
....
....
....
....
....
....
....

VICTOR MARSHALL

Emotional Health Lifestyle Scorecard

Week _____

ACTIVITY	DAY OF THE WEEK AND DATE						
	Sun --/--/--	**Mon** --/--/--	**Tues** --/--/--	**Wed** --/--/--	**Thurs** --/--/--	**Fri** --/--/--	**Sat** --/--/--
Spiritual Engagement * Prepare for the journey of restoration with spiritual practices (See *Set the Captives Free Workbook*, pp.15, 73							
Relationship Building Pray for a particular family member/relative/friend with whom you are having difficulty							
Exercise Engage in Exercise. State the type and amount of time daily							
Goal-setting Identify two or three things you wish to accomplish daily AND MONTHLY. This inspires hope and optimism in that you would have accomplished a goal							
Discussion Time * Identify any two (2) issues to be addressed with a particular family member/relative/friend, and prayerfully talk to that person about the issues							
Personal Reflection How much time have you spent on the reflection activity at the end of each **SESSION**?							
Special Reading On a daily basis, read ten (10) verses from the Gospel of St Mark 1-12. Also identify and **MEMORISE** the verse that attracts you.	*Verses Read*	*Verses Read*	*Verses Read*	*Verses Read*	*Verses Read*	*Verses Read*	*Verses Read*
Favourite Verse(s)							
Water How many glasses of water did you drink during the day?							

NOTE: * Place a tick (√) in the box next to these items to show that you have completed the activity on a daily basis. It is expected that these activities will take time and will be on-going.

NOTES

Feel free to use this space to write out the verse you are memorising from the chapter you have read this week, as a way of helping you internalise the text.

Session Six

Forgiveness: Its Healing Power (Part I1)

During this session, pay attention to:

1) Stages Three, Four and Five of the Journey towards Forgiveness.

2) The Impact of Living with unresolved past painful issues.

3) Benefits of extending forgiveness

4) Processes to be followed in order to experience emotional and spiritual healing.

5) Focus areas necessary for moving on emotionally and spiritually.

You will notice in your workbook that you have the outline of the PowerPoint presentation for **Session Six**, so that you may follow along.

DVD/PowerPoint Slides

Session Six

Forgiveness: Its Healing Power (Part I1)

During the PowerPoint presentations, feel free to follow along with the slides that correspond with those in the session. You can fill in the blank spaces with the missing words. Use the blanks in the margin with the letters that match to the letters on the blanks in the PowerPoint slides. (For example, for blank [a], write the answer on the line next to the section of the slide marked [a].

1.

> # EMOTIONAL HEALTH RESTORATION PROGRAMME
>
> Identifying Emotional Dys-functionality
> and Possible Solutions

2.

> ## Session 6
>
> Forgiveness: Its Healing Power
> (Part II)

Hindrances to High-level Wellness

Various factors affect our health and wellness. For example:

- injustice, prejudice, and unfair treatment.
- Disappointments
- One's authority, feelings or property disregarded by other.
- Ignored or treated badly by others.
- Experience of prolonged abuse, assault or harm
- unforgiveness

The Twelve 'Risk' Categories

1. Emotional Instability
2. Emotional Hurt
3. Lifestyle
4. Nutrition
5. **Unforgiveness**
6. Abuse
7. Unresolved Issues
8. Inability to Cope
9. Medical Condition
10. Childhood Adversity
11. Psychological Needs
12. Mental Functioning

Unresolved Past Issues

Individuals tend to live with unresolved past issues for two main reasons.

Such individuals:

- have not experienced _____a____ for the issues.
- are unable to ____b____ the negative emotions which emerge from the hurt.

Szasz, P. L., et al. (2011). The effect of emotion regulation strategies on anger. *Behaviour Research and Therapy,* 49 (2), 114-119, (114).

3.

4.

5.

a. _____

b. _____

Consequences of living with unresolved past painful issues

The negative impact which accompanies living with unresolved past painful issues are: re-invigorating/re-creating the negative emotions and engaging in maladaptive, counterproductive, or unhealthy behaviours. Additionally, individuals tend to undergo a hindered psychological wellbeing, experience disrupted relationships and display poor level of functionality (dysfunctional or non-functional).

Szasz et al. (2011), 'The effect of emotion regulation strategies on anger', p.114.

6.

Impact of Re-living the Past

7.

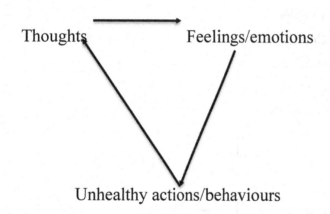

Thoughts → Feelings/emotions

Unhealthy actions/behaviours

Impact of Re-living the Unresolved Past

Thoughts produce feelings and emotions, which contribute to the _____**c**_____ being displayed. Such behaviours consolidate the thoughts circulating in the mind. Negative thoughts can create feelings and bring out negative emotions (e.g: bitterness, hostility, etc), thus resulting in _____**d**_____ actions and behaviours such as revengeful attitudes and retaliation.

8.

c. _____

d. _____

Healing Power of Forgiveness

STAGE 1 Facing unresolved past issues	→	STAGE 2 Surrender the unresolved past	→	STAGE 3 Leave the past behind

9.

Internal Resolution About Past Un-resolved Difficulties

In order to go through Stage 3 of the Journey towards Forgiveness successfully it would be beneficial to alter your _____**e**____ of the issue. This requires changing your view or belief about the situation, recognise that you have not reached the end of your journey, "but one thing *I do,* forgetting those things which are behind and reaching forward to those things which are ahead."

Philippians 3:13, NKJV.

10.

e. _____

Leave the Painful Past in the Past: Step 1

The first step in this stage involves _____**f**_____ or identifying the hindrances in your life. To do this, it is important that we take time to _____**g**_____ intentionally about where you are emotionally and engage in personal assessment of your emotional well-being. For example, what aspect of my past un-resolved issue is affecting me? How am I handling this difficult issue?

11.

f. _____

g. _____

Cognitive Restructuring

On recognising these hindrances, seek to make conscious and informed decisions, one of which is to get rid of or 'lose' these hindrances in your life. One way to achieve this is to adjust your perception by using reality-based ways of _____**h**_____ the situation differently. This approach is referred to as cognitive restructuring/re-appraisal.

Barlow, D.W. et al. (2011). *Unified Protocol for Transdiagnostic Treatment of Emotional Disorders: Therapist Guide.* (London: Oxford University Press).

Leave the Painful Past in the Past: Step 2

In proceeding through this stage, it is essential to identify a major Christ-centred _____**i**_____ which would help us with emotional, psychological and spiritual healing. For instance, some of the goals could be to:
- gain freedom from the emotionally-difficult issue.
- make peace with the perpetrator or
- extend forgiveness.

Leave the Painful Past in the Past: Step 3

The third step involves identifying a major goal and focusing on this new goal, which requires single-mindedness. This means having a single over-riding ___**j**_____, and a determined, steadfast approach to achieving that goal. The desire should also be to accomplish your specific goal. This new mindset aids you in not living in the 'past' where destructive emotional issues exist and your former pain become visible.

12.

h. _____

13.

i. _____

14.

j. _____

Graphic Illustration of the Mind

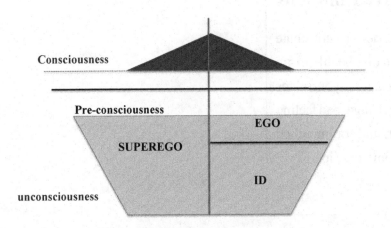

15.

The Mind	**16.**

The Mind

Forgiveness becomes more possible when individuals are contented, _____**k**_____ and settled. This type of contentment needs to be cultivated and it blossoms when your *present* situations/circumstances outweigh your past or that which you are deficient in and what you desire in the *future*.

Tibbits, D., Halliday, S. (2006). *Forgive to Live: How Forgiveness Can Save Your Life* (TN: Thomas Nelson), p.125.

16.

k. _____

Remedy for Negative Emotions

17.

Courage, hope, faith, sympathy [and] love promote health and prolong life. A contented mind, a cheerful spirit, is health to the body and strength to the soul. In the treatment of the sick the effect of mental influence should not be overlooked. Rightly used, this influence affords one of the most effective agencies for combating disease.

White, *Counsels on Health*, p.1013

Battling Against Negative Emotions

18.

The biblical counsel guides us in how to eliminate negative emotions which impact our health in an unhealthy way. .But now put away and rid yourselves [completely] of all these things: anger, rage, bad feeling toward others, curses and slander, and foulmouthed abuse and shameful utterances from your lips!

Colossians 3:8, AMP.

Physiological Health Benefits of Forgiveness

19.

Scientific research indicates that forgiveness directly improves health by reducing hostility and cardiovascular strain. It also acts as a buffer for the immune system by releasing antibodies. Furthermore, extending forgiveness improves the functioning of the central nervous system via parts of the brain such as the amygdala, and the hypothalamus.

Adina Karner-Huțuleac, (2020). Forgiveness, Unforgiveness and Health. *Journal of Intercultural Management and Ethics,* 3(2), pp.51-58 (52).

Mental Health Benefits of Forgiveness

20.

A research study involving 66 university undergraduates indicates that forgiveness is associated with positive traits such as empathy and agreeableness. The more often individuals extend forgiveness, the less depressed they felt, while less anger and hostility were displayed.

Jack W. Berry, Everett L. Worthington Jr. ,Lynn E. O'Connor , Les Parrott, Nathaniel G. Wade. (2005). Forgivingness, Vengeful Rumination, and Affective Traits. *Journal of Personality,* 73 (1), 183-226 (204, 213).

Relationship Between Forgiveness and Psychological Needs

In 2010, a study was conducted with six hundred 19 - 28 year-old Croatian students. There was a positive link between revenge and avoidance types of motivation and depression in males, while there was positive link for revenge motivation and depression in females. However, the greater the desire for revenge in males, the less happy they felt.

Rijavec, M., Jurčec, L., Mijočević, I. (2010). Gender Differences in the Relationship between Forgiveness and Depression/ Happiness. *Psihologijske teme*, 19, 1, 189-202 (195, 198).

21.

Remedy for Emotional Distress

The love which The Healing Saviour diffuses through the whole being is a vitalizing power. Every vital part--the brain, the heart, the nerves--it touches with _____l_____. By it the highest energies of the being are roused to activity. It frees the soul from the _____m_____ and sorrow, the _____n_____ and care (worries), that crush the life forces. With it come serenity and composure.

White, *Ministry of Healing*, p.115.

22.

l. _____

m. _____

n. _____

Processes for Emotional and Spiritual Healing (Stage 4)

Pave the way: One approach is to initiate connection with the perpetrator by employing a third person to engage in mediation. This allows you to face the perpetrator, with support, and where possible, to offload the emotional wounded-ness in a different form. This could occur through seeing the perpetrator and respectfully sharing about the impact of his/her behaviour on you and the pain it has caused.

Marshall, *On the Road to Forgiveness,* pp.139-143..

23.

Healing Power of Forgiveness

24.

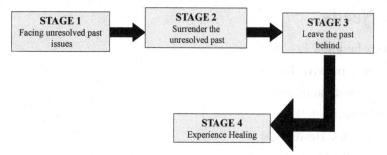

Processes for Emotional and Spiritual Healing

Self-Disclose: Seek for a transformation. With the aid of a mediator, express your view of the situation to your perpetrator, alerting him/her of your degree of hurt and how insensitive he/she has been to you. By keeping the _____**O**_____ before your perpetrator, you will be engaged in Minimal Effective Responses. Along with this, declare that you have been converted.

Marshall, *On the Road to Forgiveness,* p.145..

25.

o. _____

Biblical Counsel

The Sacred Text helps us to understand the actual Source of our healing. We are alerted that "He [*The Healing Saviour*] has borne our griefs and carried our sorrows; Yet we esteemed Him stricken, Smitten by God, and afflicted. But He *was* wounded for our transgressions, *He was* bruised for our iniquities; The chastisement for our peace *was* upon Him, And by His stripes we are healed.

Isaiah 53:4,5 (NKJV).

26.

Processes for Emotional and Spiritual Healing

Consolidate: Seek to display Christian virtues by showing compassion and empathy to others. A display of such qualities could disturb their conscience intensely to the point of bringing about guilt on their part. Additionally, reinforce the act of forgiveness by displaying a forgiving attitude and declare your willingness to move on.

27.

Processes for Emotional and Spiritual Healing

Individuals reacting with bitterness or other negative emotions are thought to be psychologically _____**p**_____. A major factor which contributes to this is an _____**q**_____ attitude or a lack of apologies. It is important to note that "Effective apologies must meet at least one psychological need of the victim, such as ... validation of the victim's emotional response to the transgression."

Aaron Lazare, *On Apology* (NY: Oxford University Press, 204), p.24

28.

p. _____

q. _____

Healing Power of Forgiveness

29.

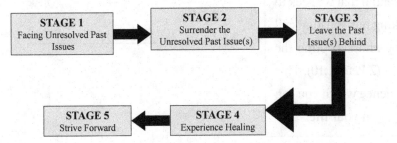

Visualize the Goal and Strive Forward

Strive Forward:

Having reached Stage 5 of the Journey towards Forgiveness, it is essential that you seek to move ahead by internalizing the biblical perspective to "press on toward the _____r___ to win the [heavenly] _____s_____ of the upward call of God in Christ Jesus, our _____t_____ Redeemer."

Phil 3:14, AMP.

30.

r. _____

s. _____

t. _____

Strive Forward

In extending forgiveness, it is essential that the bigger picture be always kept in view. This occurs by considering other essential aspects of your life such as your health, and your children's future, seeing that they are linked to emotional _____u_____, emotional progress and healing.

Nelson SK, Fuller JAK, Choi I, Lyubomirsky S. Beyond Self-Protection: Self-Affirmation Benefits Hedonic and Eudaimonic Well-Being. *Personality and Social Psychology Bulletin.* 2014;40(8):998-1011.

31.

u. _____

Moving Forward Emotionally

Moving on from emotional ___v____ and difficulties requires us to focus on a saving relationship with the Healing Redeemer and the _____w_____ which He gained at Calvary's Cross. It is essential that we seek to ensure that we have a faith by making our spiritual call and election sure and by believing and accepting the death of Christ, our Healing Saviour (2 Peter 1:10). This also entails seeking for a new experience which you can share concerning the Divine __x___ in your life.

32.

v. _____

w. _____

x. _____

Focusing on Issue of Eternal Value

An important purpose for which Christ endured the crucifixion was to _____**y**____ each human being back to the Divine Creator. We are reminded that "all things are from God, Who through *Jesus* Christ reconciled us to Himself [received us into favor, brought us into harmony with Himself] and gave to us the ministry of reconciliation [that by word and deed we might aim to bring others into harmony with Him]"

2 Cor 5:18, AMP).

33.

y. _____

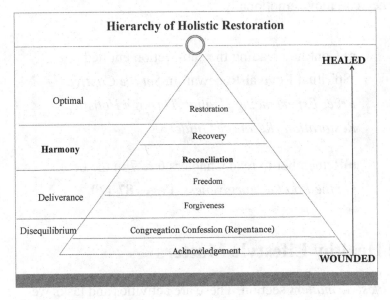

Hierarchy of Holistic Restoration

HEALED

Optimal — Restoration

Harmony — Recovery

Reconciliation

Deliverance — Freedom

Forgiveness

Disequilibrium — Congregation Confession (Repentance)

Acknowledgement

WOUNDED

34.

Focus on Issues of Eternal Value

In developing the capacity to move on emotionally and spiritually, an important step is to be aware that we are a chosen race, a royal priesthood, a holy nation, God's own people, in order that you may proclaim the mighty acts of him who called you out of darkness into his marvellous light' (1 Peter. 2: 9). This perspective assists you in learning to live a meaningful life as you focus on matters which have eternal value.

35.

Summary

➤ Leaving past painful issues in the past involves three processes: identifying hindrances, ear-marking specific goals and aspiring to fulfil one of these major goals.

➤ An essential component in seeking to leave the past painful issues in the past is pinpointing a wholesome goal.

➤ Various benefits can be derived from extending forgiveness. Some of these are physiological (e.g: building up of immune system) and mental health (e.g: less depressed).

➤ Minimal Effective Responses are needed to bring closure to an emotional hurt.

➤ Finding meaning in life and focusing on higher goals can motivate individuals to extend forgiveness so that they can move emotionally.

Insightful Perspectives

> **a)** Continue reading the sub-section entitled 'Spiritual Revival/Renewal' in *Set the Captives Free: Experiencing Healing Through Holistic Restoration (Resource Guide)*,
>
> **b)** Remember to read Chapters 6 & 7 in the book: *On the Road to Forgiveness,* **Pages 87-120.**

Emotional Healthy Lifestyle Matters

Let's turn to the *emotional healthy lifestyle matters* section. These are activities and tasks we can engage in to aid our emotional, physical, psychological, relational, social and spiritual development. Some of these can be done on your own at home.

1. Replacing Negative Views/Thoughts with Inspiring Material

Since we possess an innate disposition to think negatively of others when they injure or mistreat us, we tend to mix negative thoughts with our actions and attitudes. However, learning to replace these thoughts with inspiring material can help us move to the point of extending forgiveness, by which we can experience healing. Additionally, this act helps us to build healthy and positive **interpersonal relationships,** the fifth component of the HEALINGS health principles.

TASK 1

a) Reflect on any negative thoughts have you been focusing on in the last month/ or on any negative views you have developed or nurtured of yourself or of someone else in the last month. *Share this experience in the space below.*

....
....
....
....
....
....
....
....

TASK 2

a) **Consider this thought**

"For as he thinks in his heart, so is he. As one who reckons, he says to you, eat and drink, yet his heart is not with you [but is grudging the cost]" (Proverb 23:7, AMP).

b) How can you relate to the above text with your experience of negative thoughts?

....
....
....
....
....
....
....
....

TASK 3

a) Prayerfully read through this thought:

"For the rest, brethren, whatever is true, whatever is worthy of reverence *and* is honorable *and* seemly, whatever is just, whatever is pure, whatever is lovely *and* lovable, whatever is kind *and* winsome *and* gracious, if there is any virtue *and* excellence, if there is anything worthy of praise, think on *and* weigh *and* take account of these things [fix your minds on them]. [9] Practice what you have learned and received and heard and seen in me, *and* model your way of living on it, and the God of peace (of [e]untroubled, undisturbed well-being) will be with you" (Phil 4:8-9, AMP).

b) Although the experience was a difficult one for you, write out **two (2)** positive things that you can think of which came out of a difficult situation you had.

....

....

....

....

....

....

....

2. Building Relationships

Healthy and positive interpersonal relationships require a display of wholesome attitudes and behaviours and healthy interactions with others. One way to achieve this is to engage emotionally by working through the material relating to the Journey Towards Forgiveness. Having started the journey in **Session 5**, we will continue to explore this journey.

TASK 1:

a) In your *Set the Captives free: 12 Studies for Individuals or Groups* Workbook, on **pages 53 – 58**, you will find activities to assist you in continuing the Journey Towards Forgiveness. Work through the activities on these pages as you seek to further extend and receive forgiveness.

VICTOR MARSHALL

3. Water intake

The plasma, which is the liquid part of the blood, is 92% water. It is the main source of getting rid of excretory products and waste matter such as carbon dioxide. Since the life of the organism is in the blood, it is important to have healthy blood and a good intake of water can assist you in achieving this goal.

> **CHALLENGE:** while you are attending the session today, endeavour to drink ONE (1) half-litre bottle of water by the end of this session. This is equivalent to two (2) cups of water.

4. Goal-setting

Setting realistic goals and having the determination and motivation to pursue these personal goals contribute to individuals being inspired with hope, thus leading to living a meaningful life. The pursuit of goals affords individuals with a purpose in life and therefore, they tend to be optimistic which relates to **hope,** the first component of the HEALINGS health principles.

TASK 1:

In order to leave the painful past issues in the past, it is advisable to identify three (3) goals which can help you progress emotionally. For example, a goal could be to meet the perpetrator.

(a) Write your **three (3)** achievable, realistic goals here:

1) _____

2) _____

3) _____

TASK 2:

In learning to focus, individuals are expected to develop single-mindedness (Marshall, 2015: 101), an attribute (quality) which contributes to the mind influencing the body and one's attitude impacting on his/her health.

(a) Afterward, select your **CENTRAL/ MAJOR** goal on which you would be focusing:

_____

_____

_____

_____

5. Assessment

Turn to the Assessment and Evaluation Tools Kit and take some time to complete the **Relational Self-care and Wellness Assessment** relating to your relational health, which you started in *Session 5* on **Page 101** of this *Companion Folder.* As you work through the statements, seek to be as honest as possible and be very demanding on yourself.

Here is a useful quotation

"Higher than the highest human thought can reach is the Divine Healer's ideal for His children. Godliness – godlikeness – is the goal to be reached." White, *Education*, pp. 16-18.

Reflective Session (WEEK 6)

- **Prayerfully** reflect on **Pages 156-160 in** *On the Road to forgiveness*

1) How has this section impacted on your willingness OR unwillingness to forgive someone who has hurt you? What would you need in order to reach the stage where you can extend forgiveness, if applicable to you?

....

....

....

....

....

....

....

....

- **Read Pages 160-162 in** *On the Road to forgiveness.*

2) What progress have you made in relation to forgiveness at this point, if applicable to you? How helpful is this section of the chapter to you?

....

....

....

....

....

....

....

....

- **Read Pages 163-165 in *On the Road to forgiveness.***

3) How would you address any of the issues discussed in these few pages?

....

....

....

....

....

....

....

....

....

....

....

....

....

....

....

....

....

....

....

....

....

....

....

....

VICTOR MARSHALL

Emotional Health Lifestyle Scorecard

Week _____

ACTIVITY	DAY OF THE WEEK AND DATE						
	Sun ----/----/----	Mon ----/----/----	Tues ----/----/----	Wed ----/----/----	Thurs ----/----/----	Fri ----/----/----	Sat ----/----/----
Spiritual Engagement * Prepare for the journey of restoration with spiritual practices (See *Set the Captives Free Workbook*, pp.15, 73							
Relationship Building Pray for a particular family member/relative/friend with whom you are having difficulty							
Exercise Engage in Exercise. State the type and amount of time daily							
Goal-setting Identify two or three things you wish to accomplish daily AND MONTHLY. This inspires hope and optimism in that you would have accomplished a goal							
Discussion Time * Identify any two (2) issues to be addressed with a particular family member/relative/friend, and prayerfully talk to that person about the issues							
Personal Reflection How much time have you spent on the reflection activity at the end of each **SESSION**?							
Special Reading On a daily basis, read ten (10) verses from the Gospel of St Mark 1-12. Also identify and **MEMORISE** the verse that attracts you.	*Verses Read*	*Verses Read*	*Verses Read*	*Verses Read*	*Verses Read*	*Verses Read*	*Verses Read*
Favourite Verse(s)	....	....	....	....	....	....	....
Water How many glasses of water did you drink during the day?							

NOTE: * Place a tick (√) in the box next to these items to show that you have completed the activity on a daily basis. It is expected that these activities will take time and will be on-going.

NOTES

Feel free to use this space to write out the verse you are memorising from the chapter you have read this week, as a way of helping you internalise the text.

Session Seven

A Journey to the Underworld

During this session, pay attention to:

1) The concept of emotional freedom

2) The five (5) Stages in the Journey towards Emotional Freedom

3) Impact and purposes of emotional strongholds

4) Gaining victory over strongholds

You will notice in your workbook that you have the outline of the PowerPoint presentation for **Session Seven**, so that you may follow along.

Session Seven

A Journey to the Underworld

During the PowerPoint presentations, feel free to follow along with the slides that correspond with those in the session. You can fill in the blank spaces with the missing words. Use the blanks in the margin with the letters that match to the letters on the blanks in the PowerPoint slides. (For example, for blank [a], write the answer on the line next to the section of the slide marked [a].

1.

> # EMOTIONAL HEALTH RESTORATION PROGRAMME
>
> Identifying Emotional Dys-functionality and Possible Solutions

2.

> ### Session 7
>
> ### A Journey to the Underworld

Emotional freedom:

The ability to love [others] by cultivating _____**a**_____ emotions and being able to compassionately witness and _____**b**_____ negative ones, whether they are yours or belonging to another person.

Judith Orloff, (2009). *Emotional Freedom: Liberate Yourself from Negative Emotions and Transform Your Life* (NY: Harmony Books), p.2.

Definitions

The power to be yourself and to _____**c**_____ your life without being restricted by other forces. It is the ____**d**____ to live your life without being dragged down by toxic or negative emotions.

Steve Wells & David Lake, *Enjoy Emotional Freedom: Simple Techniques for Living Life to the Full* (Wollombi, NSW: Exisle Publishing, 2010), p.7..

Examples of Strongholds

Difficulties such as abuse, _____**e**_____, bitterness, unwholesome cultural habits, guilt and shame are referred to as _____ **f** _____ or fortresses or prisons. They contribute to particular _____**g**_____ and processes that instigate people to behave and respond in emotionally destructive ways. These strongholds have the capacity to affect one's inner peace and wellbeing.

Topper, C. J. & Koenig, H. G. (2012). *Spirituality in Pastoral Counseling and the Community Helping Professions* (NY: Routledge), p. 145.

3.

a. _____

b. _____

4.

c. _____

d. _____

5.

e. _____

f. _____

g. _____

The Twelve 'Risk' Categories

1. Emotional Instability
2. Emotional Hurt
3. Lifestyle
4. Nutrition
5. Unforgiveness
6. Abuse
7. **Unresolved Issues**
8. Inability to Cope
9. Medical Condition
10. Childhood Adversity
11. Psychological Needs
12. Mental Functioning

Biblical Perspective on Strongholds

For though we walk in the flesh, we do not war according to the flesh. For the weapons of our warfare *are* not carnal but mighty in the Almighty One for pulling down strongholds, casting down arguments and every high thing that exalts itself against the knowledge of the Creator of the Universe, bringing every thought into captivity to the obedience of Christ, the Healing Redeemer and being ready to punish all disobedience when your obedience is fulfilled.

(2 Cor 10:3-6, NKJV)

Types of Negative strongholds

Spiritual (evil, territorial). An example is adversity/affliction which is a condition that causes anguish, distress and _____**h**_____ and can also be of a financial or physical nature. Additionally, evil forces can exist in homes, organisations and communities, indicating that there are evil forces existing or functioning around us in our external environment.

Eph 6:12

6.

7.

8.

h. _____

Types of Strongholds

Mental/psychological: These relate to holding on to a set of negative _____i_____ or mental thoughts; negative ideological views which are unwholesome. For example, being suspicious or unwilling to trust anyone, displaying prejudice towards others, and stigmatizing individuals.

Types of Strongholds: Emotional

Personal/relational: These types of strongholds consist of negative _____j_____, _____k_____ and _____l_____ which we develop unconsciously. These actions and behaviours result in difficulties such as apathy (lack of interest in matters of importance), and isolation which contribute to individuals being lethargic/ lifeless, hopeless and pessimistic.

Research Evidence

A study involving 76 adults, age 18 -35, found that individuals who identified their thoughts as more negative, and/or less detailed, scored higher on areas of poor psychological wellbeing such as depression. Therefore, negative thinking does not benefit our emotional health.

Andrews-Hanna JR, Kaiser RH, Turner AEJ, Reineberg AE, Godinez D, Dimidjian S and Banich MT (2013) A penny for your thoughts: dimensions of self-generated thought content and relationships with individual differences in emotional wellbeing. *Frontiers in Psychology,* 4(900).

9.

i. _____

10.

j. _____

k. _____

l. _____

11.

Insight

The work of gaining salvation is one of co-partnership, a joint operation. There is to be co-operation between the [Divine Creator] and the repentant sinner. This is necessary for the formation of right principles in the character. Man is to make earnest efforts to overcome that which hinders him from attaining to perfection. But he is wholly dependent upon the [Divine Creator] for success. Human effort of itself is not sufficient.

White, *Acts of the Apostles,* p. 482.

12.

Source of Strongholds

Identify the Root: Since the Divine Creator has intended that we be emotionally whole and be free from the impact of negative emotions, we are reminded that " God has not given us a spirit of _____**m**_____ and timidity, but of _____**n**_____, love, and self-discipline"

(2 Tim 1:7).

13.

m. _____

n. _____

Effects of Strongholds

These strongholds are strategies being used to defeat us and ultimately lead to the development of poor ___**o**___ esteem and low self- _____**p**_____. A reversal of this situation can be experienced through various ways. One approach is believing in and accepting the _____**q**_____ which Christ, our Healing Redeemer, has gained on Calvary's Cross.

14.

o. _____

p. _____

q. _____

Biblical Counsel

Identifying the Resources: The spiritual resources are our experience of salvation, ___**r**___, Gospel of peace, ____**s**____, righteousness, and truth, which is the Sacred Scriptures. These are divinely established to destroy/pull down/detach/demolish strongholds. Additionally they refute and destroy hostile _____**t**_____ towards individuals.

Eph 6:16-18; 2 Cor 10:4-6

15.

r. _____

s. _____

t. _____

A Five-stage Process for Addressing Unresolved Underlying Issues

16.

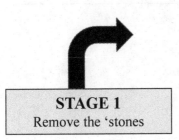

STAGE 1
Remove the 'stones

Insight

White, in one of her works, insightfully shared that "He *[the Healing Redeemer]* saw that in the history of the world, beginning with the death of Abel, the conflict between good and evil had been unceasing... He saw the suffering and sorrow, tears and death, that were to be the lot of men. His heart was pierced with the ___**u**____ of the human family of all ages and in all lands. The woes of the sinful race were heavy upon His soul, and the fountain of His tears was broken up as He longed to relieve all their distress."

White, *Desire of Ages,* p.534.

17.

u. _____

Divine Command

With a Divine desire to relieve human distress, "Jesus, *[our Healing Saviour]* again deeply moved within [to the point of anger], approached the tomb. It was a cave, and a boulder was lying against it [to cover the entrance]." Having braced himself and armed with Holy boldness and divine wrath over our emotional difficulties, Jesus said, "Take away the stone."

John 11:38-39 (AMP)

18.

Stage I: Process for Addressing Unresolved Underlying Issues

This stage requires us to remove the emotional 'stones' in our lives. These are seen as _____**v**_____, which hinder emotional progress. They are based on past negative and hurtful experiences which consist of unresolved issues, unwholesome/undesirable behaviours/patterns and negative mental beliefs which contribute to self-defeat.

Marshall, V. D. (2013). *Set the captives free: Experiencing healing through holistic restoration* (Bloomington, IN: AuthorHouse), p.48.

19.

v. _____

Examples of Emotional Blockages

Some of these blockages are negative emotions such as anger, envy and guilt; and negative feelings such as shame. They act as defensive ____**w**_____ to cope with deep emotional pain which has occurred in:
- traumatic, and
- dysfunctional situations such as abuse or betrayal.

20.

w. _____

Five Ways to Break the Barriers

- Select, read and meditate on relevant biblical texts for your situation.
- Engage in daily intercessory prayer about the
- _____**x**_____.
- Avoid ____ **y**_____ talk and pessimistic people.
- Follow the therapeutic counsel and the Divine guidance from the biblical texts.
- Adopt the 'boomerang' prayer by using relevant biblical texts in praying them back to the Healing Saviour of all human beings.

21.

x. _____

y. _____

Scientific Evidence

A study involving 109 individuals, aged 65+ indicated that pessimism may play an essential role in older adults who experienced illness-related anxiety. Additionally, when facing medical illness, pessimistic health expectations (e.g: fear of relapse, symptoms worsening, or death) and pessimistic psychological expectations (e.g: fear of role changes or loss of social interaction) tend to contribute more strongly to the presence of anxiety.

Hirsch, J., Walker, K., Chang, E., & Lyness, J. (2012). Illness burden and symptoms of anxiety in older adults: Optimism and pessimism as moderators. International Psychogeriatrics, 24(10), 1614-1621.

22.

Stage 2: Addressing Unresolved Underlying Issues

23.

| STAGE 1 Remove the 'stones | → | STAGE 2 Create a Conducive Environment |

Create a Conducive Environment

Assess your internal environment to address issues such as:

- grief,
- helplessness, and hopelessness.

Also examine the external environment to eliminate negativity such as annoyance, and unhappiness. Negative emotions and feelings are indicators that there are _____**z**_____around us.

24.

z. _____

Scientific Evidence

1078 workers, age 26-65, were in a study, with 55% operating in shared and 45% in open-plan offices. It focused on the impact of irrelevant speech noise on areas such as annoyance, performance, and mental health. Results showed that:

- 69% of those in shared offices and
- 66% of the open-plan employees declared a loss of concentration from noise.

Employees in open-plan offices expressed symptoms such as being less motivated and tiredness, more than those in shared offices.

Di Blasio S, Shtrepi L, Puglisi GE, Astolfi A. A Cross-Sectional Survey on the Impact of Irrelevant Speech Noise on Annoyance, Mental Health and Well-being, Performance and Occupants' Behavior in Shared and Open-Plan Offices. *International Journal of Environmental Research and Public Health.* 2019; 16(2):280.

25.

Insightful Counsel

It is not only our privilege but our duty to cultivate gentleness, to have the peace of Christ in the heart .... [*We*] may possess many good and useful qualities; but their characters are greatly marred by an unkind, fretful, fault-finding, harshly judging temper. The husband or the wife who cherishes suspicion and distrust creates dissension and strife in the home. Neither of them should keep his gentle words and smiles for strangers alone, and manifest irritability in the home, thus driving out peace and contentment.

White, E. G. (2000). *Mind, Character & Personality Vol. 2* (Hagerstown, MD: Review & Herald Publishing Association), p.156

26.

Stage 3: Addressing Unresolved Underlying Issues

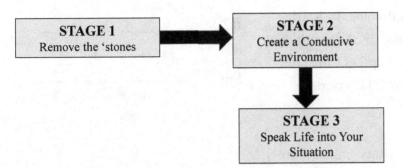

27.

Stage 3: Invigoration

Another process in accomplishing emotional freedom is to be invigorated on various levels:

- emotional,

- physical and

- spiritual.

Ancient wisdom teaches that "the _____**a2**_____ can bring death or life; those who love to talk will reap the consequences."

Proverbs 18:21, NLT

28.

a2._____

Power of Words (I)

Use uplifting words to impart life into your being. Your spoken words can affect another person's feelings, and _____**b2**_____. Individuals cannot control reality from their words but what they say can affect others, by hurting their:

- emotions or

- _____**c2**_____ them up.

Marshall, *Set the captives free: Experiencing healing through holistic restoration*, p.49.

29.

b2._____

c2._____

Ancient Guidance

Ancient writing counsels that "faith comes by hearing [what is told], and what is heard comes by the preaching [of the message that came from the lips] of Christ (the Messiah Himself): [Rom 10:17, AMP] Conversely,

- denial,
- distrust, doubt,
- suspicion and uncertainty also are _____d2_____ by hearing _____e2_____ ideas, perspectives, thoughts, and views.

30.

d2. _____

e2. _____

Accentuate the Positive I

Having a positive mindset improves our emotional well-being. For example, encouragement comes from these Ancient words: "Why are you cast down, O my inner self? And why should you moan over me *and* be disquieted within me? Hope in God *and* wait expectantly for Him, for I shall yet praise Him, Who is the help of my countenance, and my God."

Psalm 42:11, AMP)

31.

Stage 4: Addressing Unresolved Underlying Issues

32.

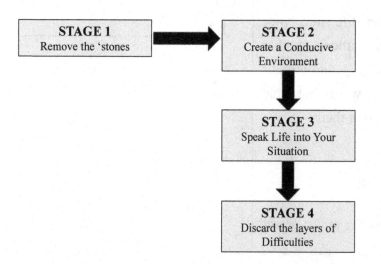

Unwrap unwholesome Emotional Layers

Stage 4 in this journey involves discarding layers of emotional difficulties such as apathy, low self-esteem, rejection and a sense of unworthiness. Individuals, through counselling and therapy, would need to revise:
- old mindsets,
- unlearn wrong, health-destroying habits and
- re-programme their minds to adopt _____**f2**_____ lifestyles.

Marshall, *Set the captives free: Experiencing healing through holistic restoration*, p.50.

33.

f2._____

Stage 5: Addressing Unresolved Underlying Issues

34.

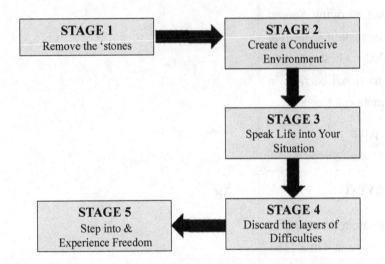

Step into and Experience Freedom

At this stage of the journey, it is essential that you take on a new _____**g2**_____. This involves behaving, speaking and thinking as a liberated individual. Additionally, conduct yourself confidently knowing that 'if the Son makes you free, then you are unquestionably free' (Jn 8:36, AMP).

Marshall, *Set the captives free: Experiencing healing through holistic restoration*, p.51.

35.

g2._____

Mental Transformation

36.

Strip yourselves of your former nature [put off and discard your old unrenewed self] which characterized your previous manner of life and becomes corrupt through lusts *and* desires that spring from delusion; And be constantly renewed in the spirit of your mind [having a fresh mental and spiritual attitude], And put on the new nature (the regenerate self) created in God's image, [Godlike] in true righteousness and holiness.

Ephesians 4:22, AMP

High Spiritual Esteem

37.

h2._____

Building a high spiritual esteem can occur when we engage continually in spiritual disciplines or practices such as meditation, theological reflection and studying Sacred Scriptures. This helps us to develop or sustain a spiritual ____**h2**____ with the Divine Saviour. These positive spiritual activities can replace the emotional barriers in our life, thereby, consolidating our emotional freedom.

Marshall, *On the Road to Forgiveness,* p.188

Freedom Achieved

38.

Freedom has been gained for us and we are reminded of it, in that Christ, the Healing Redeemer, indicated that "The Spirit of the Creator of the world [is] upon Me, because He has anointed Me [the Anointed One, the Messiah] to preach the good news (the Gospel) to the poor; He has sent Me to announce release to the captives and recovery of sight to the blind, to send forth as delivered those who are oppressed [who are downtrodden, bruised, crushed, and broken down by calamity]" Through this Divine work, we can experience the freedom be it emotional, psychological or spiritual.

(Lk 4:18, AMP)

Summary

> Individuals experience emotional freedom when they are in control of an emotionally difficult situation

> Negative strongholds act like prisons and keep individuals stuck at different levels.

> Negative strongholds are categorised as spiritual, emotional or mental (psychological)

> Spiritual disciplines such as studying the Word of God and meditation help individuals form a high spiritual esteem

> The spiritual disciplines are effective through divine power in overcoming the negative strongholds

Insightful Perspectives

> **a)** Remember to take some time to go through the Section entitled 'A Journey Towards Total Freedom' on **pages 45-48** in *Set the Captives Free (Resource Guide).*
>
> **b)**Turn to Chapter 6 and engage in the week's reading –'Fading Hope' in *Raising the Wounded: Grasping for Hope in the Midst of Despair.*

Emotional Healthy Lifestyle Matters

Let's turn to the *emotional healthy lifestyle matters* section. These are activities and tasks we can engage in to aid our emotional, physical, psychological, relational, social and spiritual development. Some of these can be done on your own at home.

1. Building Spiritual esteem

Spiritual esteem is a component of spiritual wellbeing and aids in promoting one's spiritual health. Additionally, it is an aspect of **Spiritual Guidance,** the seventh component of the HEALINGS health principles. In order to experience positive spiritual wellbeing, individuals need to build their spiritual esteem.

TASK 1

Select another person from the group and connect with him/her for 3 days. Spend five (5) minutes, each day, reciting this affirmative statement to your partner, while listening to soft music.

a) I can achieve the things I desire in my life through the power of Christ who died for me on the Cross.

2. Paving the Path for Emotional Freedom

It is one thing to be aware of the various issues such as isolation, rejection and shame which bring about captivity in our life. However, to experience freedom or liberation from these issues require tools, and resources which can enable us to break and unwrap them. One way to achieve this is to engage emotionally by working through the material relating to the Journey Towards Freedom which we will commence in this **Session**.

TASK 1:

a) In your *Set the Captives free: 12 Studies for Individuals or Groups* Workbook, on **pages 59 – 65**, you will find activities to assist you in taking the Journey Towards Freedom. Work through the activities on these pages as you seek to experience liberation from various types of emotional issues.

3. Learn to Accomplish Emotional Freedom

Think of an issue you are still struggling with at present. On the other hand, it could be a person with whom you are having difficulties with at present. Read through **John 11:38-44** prayerfully.

Then Jesus, again groaning in Himself, came to the tomb. It was a cave, and a stone lay against it. Jesus said, "Take away the stone." Martha, the sister of him who was dead, said to Him, "Lord, by this time there is a stench, for he has been *dead* four days." Jesus said to her, "Did I not say to you that if you would believe you would see the glory of God?" Then they took away the stone [d]*from the place* where the dead man was lying. And Jesus lifted up *His* eyes and said, "Father, I thank You that You have heard Me. And I know that You always hear Me, but because of the people who are standing by I said *this,* that they may believe that You sent Me." Now when He had said these things, He cried with a loud voice, "Lazarus, come forth!" And he who had died came out bound hand and foot with graveclothes, and his face was wrapped with a cloth. Jesus said to them, "Loose him, and let him go" **(Jn 11:38-44)**

TASK 1

Having read through the biblical text above:

a) Identify the 'stone' which is hindering you from progressing emotionally or spiritually.

....

....

....

....

b) Describe the stench/unpleasant odour which this issue is producing.

....

....

....

....

....

c) Share what has died in your life since experiencing this issue.

....

....

....

....

....

4. Breaking Emotional Barriers (strongholds)

Each of us can identify negative attitudes, irrational beliefs, adverse situations, destructive patterns, undesirable habits, and unwholesome thoughts which have a negative impact on our life. When these elements persist frequently and impact us beyond our control, they are classified as strongholds which need to be broken or emotional layers which need unwrapping in order to experience emotional freedom.

TASK 1

a) Take a few moments and list at least three (3) strongholds which you would like to break.

....

....

....

....

b) How eager are you to break the strongholds listed above? On a scale of 0 to 10, where 0 is not eager and 10 is 'extremely eager', mark each stronghold above with a number rating.

0	1	2	3	4	5	6	7	8	9	10

Not Eager   **Eager**   **Extremely Eager**

....

....

....

VICTOR MARSHALL

TASK 2

a) Select the two (2) strongholds with the **highest scores** and complete the next task to put a plan in place.

....

....

....

....

....

....

....

TASK 3: Plans & Goal Setting

On the lines below, write out **a plan of how you will break each stronghold or unwrap the emotional 'layers'** in order for you to experience emotional freedom.

a) Starting today, choose the greatest emotional barrier or deepest emotional layer you would like to break or unwrap.

Today, on...20......, I will break...........................
(emotional barrier). The second barrier I desire to break is ....
I plan to do this on ....20........

b) Review the suggestions in *Slides 18-38* in this Session. Revise them daily, while working on your plan. During the upcoming days, practise them regularly and faithfully.

....

....

....

....

....

....

VICTOR MARSHALL

Reflective Prayer Session (WEEK 7)

Prayerfully Reflect on the text below.

"The Spirit of the LORD is upon me,

    for he has anointed me to bring Good News to the poor.

He has sent me to proclaim that captives will be released,

    that the blind will see,

    that the oppressed will be set free,

    and that the time of the LORD's favor [sic] has come."

                             _____ (Lk 4:18-19, NLT)

- Having read the text above, write down three (3) pastoral tasks for which Jesus was anointed.

....

....

....

....

....

....

- How can the anointing of Christ, the Healing Saviour of the human beings, help individuals who are in emotional, psychological or spiritual bondage?

....

....

....

....

....

....

- Share how any of the pastoral tasks you identified above can help you unwrap the emotional 'layers' of your hurtful situation?

....

....

....

....

....

....

....

....

....

....

....

- Spend some time praying about your layers of emotional difficulties and how this text can help you.

....

....

....

....

....

....

....

....

....

....

VICTOR MARSHALL

Emotional Health Lifestyle Scorecard

Week _____

ACTIVITY	Sun ---/----/----	Mon ---/----/----	Tues ---/----/----	Wed ---/----/---	Thurs ---/----/---	Fri ---/----/---	Sat ---/----/---
Spiritual Engagement * Prepare for the journey of restoration with spiritual practices (See *Set the Captives Free Workbook*, pp.15, 73							
Relationship Building Pray for a particular family member/relative/ friend with whom you are having difficulty							
Exercise Engage in Exercise. State the type and amount of time daily							
Goal-setting Identify two or three things you wish to accomplish daily AND MONTHLY. This inspires hope and optimism in that you would have accomplished a goal							
Discussion Time * Identify any two (2) issues to be addressed with a particular family member/relative/friend, and prayerfully talk to that person about the issues							
Personal Reflection How much time have you spent on the reflection activity at the end of each **SESSION**?							
Special Reading On a daily basis, read ten (10) verses from the Gospel of St Mark 1-12. Also identify and **MEMORISE** the verse that attracts you. .... *Favourite Verse(s)*	*Verses Read*	*Verses Read*	*Verses Read*	*Verses Read*	*Verses Read*	*Verses Read*	*Verses Read* ....
Water How many glasses of water did you drink during the day?							

The header row spanning days reads: **DAY OF THE WEEK AND DATE**

NOTE: * Place a tick (√) in the box next to these items to show that you have completed the activity on a daily basis. It is expected that these activities will take time and will be on-going.

NOTES

Feel free to use this space to write out the verse you are memorising from the chapter you have read this week, as a way of helping you internalise the text

Session Eight

Coping Strategies for Emotional Ill-health

During this session, pay attention to:

1) Prevalence of mental disorders

2) Impact of chronic and non-communicable diseases on emotional well-being

3) The three (3) categories of coping strategies

You will notice in your workbook that you have the outline of the PowerPoint presentation for **Session Eight**, so that you may follow along.

DVD/PowerPoint Slides

Session Eight

Coping Strategies for Emotional Ill-health

During the PowerPoint presentations, feel free to follow along with the slides that correspond with those in the session. You can fill in the blank spaces with the missing words. Use the blanks in the margin with the letters that match to the letters on the blanks in the PowerPoint slides. (For example, for blank [g2], write the answer on the line next to the section of the slide marked [g2].

1.

> # EMOTIONAL HEALTH RESTORATION PROGRAMME
>
> Identifying Emotional Dys-functionality and Possible Solutions

2.

> ### Session 2
>
> ### Coping Strategies for Emotional Ill-health

There are various factors which impact on our capacity to cope with emotional difficulties. For example:

- biological: genetics
- Physiological (e.g: long-term health conditions)
- Psychological: _____a_____ unresolved or untreated childhood abuse, trauma or violence
- Social (e.g: death of a close person, _____b_____, unemployment)
- Spiritual (e.g: prolonged unforgiveness)

These issues, if left unresolved tend to lead to emotional _____c_____ in our lives

3.

a. _____

b. _____

c. _____

Social Sources of Life's Difficulties

Individuals who experience difficulties could ____d___ to cope with their _____e_____ social environment such as cultural practices and socio-economic status. Interaction in this type of environment reveals personal differences in relation to exposure to and the handling of major life events such as relationship break-ups and chronic difficulties, one of which is marital problems.

Monroe, S. M., Slavich, G. M., Georgiades, K. (2009). The Social Environment and life stress in depression'. In I. H. Gotlib & C. L. Hammen (eds), *Handbook of Depression*, 2nd edn (NY: The Guildford Press), 340- 360 (341).

4.

d. _____

e. _____

Coping Skill: Resilience

In order to cope with the varying difficulties, it is important for individuals to develop ____f_____. It is the ability to properly _____g_____ to stress and adversity, which can come in the shape of family or relationship problems, health problems, or financial worries, among others. This is indicative that we are influenced (*positively or negatively*) by our social environment.

Monroe et al., 'The Social Environment and life stress in depression', p. 341.

5.

f. _____

g. _____

The Twelve 'Risk' Categories

1. Emotional Instability	7. Unresolved Issues
2. Emotional Hurt	8. **Inability to Cope**
3. Lifestyle	9. Medical Condition
4. Nutrition	10. Childhood Adversity
5. Unforgiveness	11. Psychological Needs
6. Abuse	12. Mental Functioning

6.

What is Mental health

Mental health is described as a "state of well-being in which the individual realizes his or her own _____**h**_____, can cope with the normal stresses of life, can _____**i**_____ productively and fruitfully, and is able to make a contribution to his or her community."

World Health Organization. (2013). *Comprehensive mental health action plan 2013-2020* (Geneva: WHO;[cited 2014 Jan 31], p. 12. Availablefrom: http://apps.who.int/iris/bitstream/10665/89966/1/9789241506021_eng.pdf?ua=1

7.

h. _____

i. _____

Statistical Situation: ____**j**____

In the Latin America and the Caribbean Region, 65,000 people die from suicide annually. It represents the:

- 3rd leading cause of __**k**__ for the 20 - 24 year olds,
- 4th leading factor for death in the 10 - 19 and 25 – 44 year olds.

Individuals, aged 70 + has the highest rate of suicide (12.4 per 100,000 population).

Pan American Health Organization. (2014). *Plan of Action on Mental Health 2015-2020* (Washington: PAHO). Accessed 5 November, 2021. https://www.paho.org/hq/dmdocuments/2015/plan-of-action-on-MH-2014.pdf..

8.

j. _____

k. _____

Prevalence of Chronic Diseases

Cancer is the second leading cause of death in the Caribbean Region. Care and _____**l**___ of this medical issue are needed in the small island nations of the Caribbean. The prominent type in men is prostate cancer, while breast cancer is the most common in women. Preventable illnesses such as cervical cancer, is the second leading cause of death in women in many Caribbean countries. The death rate from these cancers in the Caribbean is among the highest in the world.

Andall-Brereton, G., Bromfield, B., Smith, S. and Spence, D. (2020). Cancer Care in the Commonwealth Caribbean in COVID Times. *The Lancet*, 21(8), 1007-1009 (1007).

Impact of NCDs on Emotional Health: Diabetes

Diabetics are challenged with daily self-management such as
- frequent blood glucose monitoring, insulin administration, and physical activity.

They are burdened also with medical and financial demands daily T1D self-management. Emotional ____**m**___ such as depression, emotional distress and stress are common and contribute to the overall burden of living with T1D.

Hilliard, M. E., De Wit, M., Wasserman, R. M., Butler, A. M., Evans, M., Weissberg-Benchell, J. and Anderson, B. J. (2018). Screening and support for emotional burdens of youth with type 1 diabetes: Strategies for diabetes care providers. *Pediatric Diabetes*, 19(30), 534-543.

Emotional Health and Hypertension

A study was conducted to examine the mental health of 400 Ghanaian outpatients with hypertension, aged 18+ - 70+. Findings indicate that 57% of the outpatients experienced moderate to extremely severe ____**n**____ of anxiety. This result supports other research which found a high prevalence of anxiety among hypertensive patients in various countries such as South Africa, China and Argentina. This reveals the presence of anxiety among hypertensive patients in spite of cultural variability.

Irene A Kretchy1,2*, Frances T Owusu-Daaku1 and Samuel A Danquah (2014). Mental health in hypertension: assessing symptoms of anxiety, depression and stress on anti-hypertensive medication adherence. *International Journal of Mental Health Systems*, 8 (25).

9.

l. _____

10.

m. _____

11.

n. _____

Emotional Health and Hypertension (II)

Of the 400 outpatients, 41.5% was aged 60+, 20.5% of them had hypertension for more than 10 years and 42% had co-morbidities. One-fifth of the outpatients in the study was moderately to extreme severely ____o____. A probable explanation is that patients, showing stress symptoms, tend to be battling with co-morbidities, aging, and ____p____ with the disease for a prolonged period of time. They may have experienced negative effects of their medications which could have resulted in them discontinuing the medication.

Kretchy et al., Mental health in hypertension: assessing symptoms of anxiety, depression and stress on anti-hypertensive medication adherence.

12.

o. _____

p. _____

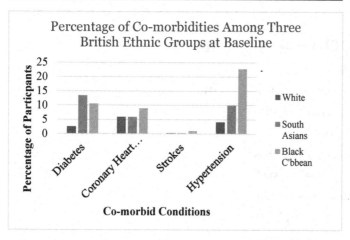

Percentage of Co-morbidities Among Three British Ethnic Groups at Baseline

NB: The study was conducted by Williams, Tillin, Richards et al. (2015). Depressive symptoms are doubled in older British South Asian and Black Caribbean people compared with Europeans: associations with excess co-morbidity and socioeconomic disadvantage. *Psychological Medicine*, 45(9), 1861–1871. However, the graph was constructed b y the author of this volume.

13.

Impact of Co-morbidities on Emotional _q__

1289 participants, aged 40-69, from a tri-ethnic cohort study were studied. Of these, At least a quarter was from each ethnic group of White European, South Asian and Black Caribbean. Overall, more Blacks suffered from co-morbidities (43.1%) than any other ethnic group. Specifically, more South Asians were diabetics than any other ethnic group, while more Blacks suffered from coronary heart disease and hypertension.

Williams, E. D., Tillin, T., Richards, M., Tuson, C., Chaturvedi, N., Hughes, A. D. and Stewart, R. (2015). Depressive symptoms are doubled in older British South Asian and Black Caribbean people compared with Europeans: associations with excess co-morbidity and socioeconomic disadvantage. *Psychological Medicine*, 45(9), 1861–1871 (1866).

14.

q. _____

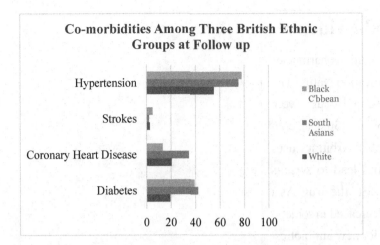

Co-morbidities Among Three British Ethnic Groups at Follow up

- Black C'bbean
- South Asians
- White

NB: **The study was conducted by** Williams, Tillin, Richards et al. (2015). Depressive symptoms are doubled in older British South Asian and Black Caribbean people compared with Europeans. However, the graph was constructed b y the author of this volume.

Impact of Co-morbidities on Emotional Health

An analysis of the follow-up data of the 1289 participants in the tri-ethnic study, indicated that more Blacks had comorbidities such as coronary heart disease and hypertension. Additionally, more Blacks presented with depression symptoms (17.7%) and stressful life events (59.7%). The major contributing factor for these symptoms among the Blacks is ___r___ disadvantage, along with psychosocial and behavioural factors among others.

Williams, et al., Depressive symptoms are doubled in older British South Asian and Black Caribbean people compared with Europeans: associations with excess co-morbidity and socioeconomic disadvantage, p.1867.

Medications and their Effects

Extensive research in the field of psychopharmacology have led to the development of several types of medications which have improved the quality of life of many individuals who suffer from different ___s___ illnesses such as bipolar disorders and depression. This positive effect of new drugs on the market still requires ongoing evaluation, in order to achieve a balance between ____t_____ effects and adverse side-effects.

Farinde, A. (2013). Brief examination of psychopharmacology. *Journal of Basic and Clinical Pharmacy,* 4(2), 49-50 (49).

15.

16.

r. _____

17.

s. _____

t. _____

Psycho-pharmacological Evidence

18.

208 patients, aged 15 – 54+, referred to Iranian pharmacies were interviewed about their self-medication status. The findings indicate that the most consumed drugs were painkillers (36.5%), followed by antibiotics (30.8%), cold medicines (16.8%), and sedatives (11.5%). Arbitrary uses of prescribed drugs such as antibiotics lead to serious side-effects including increase resistance to the drug. As a result, the usefulness of antibiotics is decreased in society, thereby leading to an increasing need for new antibiotics.

Hayati, H., Khosravi, B., Kebriaeezadeh, A., and Khanizade, M. (2015). Study of self-medication status among referring patients to Kashan pharmacies. *Journal of Pharmacoeconomics and Pharmaceutical Management,* 1(2), 45-48 (47).

Types of Coping Strategies: Adaptive

19.

Individuals use adaptive responses to manage emotional issues such as acute stress disorder, post-traumatic stress disorder and suicide, in a way that enhances their physical and psychological well-being. Accepting situations, positive reappraisal (reframing) of issues, perspective placement and social support are examples of adaptive coping strategies.

Freire, C., Mar Ferradás, M. D., Valle, A., José, C. Núñez, J. C. and Vallejo, G. (2016). Profiles of Psychological Well-being and Coping Strategies among University Students. *Frontiers in Psychology.*

Adaptive Coping and Pandemic Distress

20.

x. _____

786 participants from a Swiss longitudinal project were assessed at age 22 in relation to coping strategies used for emotional distress during the COVID-19 pandemic. Strategies such as keeping a daily routine, engaging in physical activity/exercise, seeking _____**x**_____ help, and keeping in contact with family and friends contributed to the reduction of emotional distress (e.g: perceived stress, internalizing symptoms, and anger).

Shanahan L, Steinhoff A, Bechtiger L, Murray AL, Nivette A, Hepp U, Ribeaud D, Eisner M (2020). Emotional distress in young adults during the COVID-19 pandemic: evidence of risk and resilience from a longitudinal. y. *Psychological Medicine 1–10.*

Types of Coping Strategies: Maladaptive Strategies

Maladaptive coping strategies such as aggressive behaviour, avoiding contact with people, self-blame and withdrawal exert very little _____y_____ long-term impact on stressful situations. These approaches, along with catastrophizing, and ruminating, can potentially have a negative _____z_____ on the development of interpersonal relationships.

Panahi, S., Yunus, A. S. M., Roslan, S., Kadir, R. A., Jaafar, W. M. W., and Panahi, M. S. (2016). Predictors of Psychological Well-Being among Malaysian Graduates. *The European Journal of Social and Behavioural Sciences*, 16, 2067-2083 (2069).

21.

y. _____

z. _____

Maladaptive Strategies and Young Adults

Researchers interviewed 964 participants in a New Zealand Longitudinal Study on wellbeing and coping styles at age 32 years. The research examined the impact of tobacco smoking on coping styles in adulthood. Results indicated that tobacco smoking was a more frequently used maladaptive coping strategy in dealing with problems. Furthermore, this coping strategy also reduced participants' confidence in their ability to act in a given situation.

Rob McGee, Sheila Williams,, Shyamala Nada-Raja, Craig A. Olsson. (2013). Tobacco Smoking in Adolescence Predicts Maladaptive Coping Styles in Adulthood, *Nicotine & Tobacco Research*, 15 (12), 1971–1977 (1975).

22.

Emotion- and Problem-solving-focused Strategies

Coping represents the thoughts and actions that individuals use to deal with stressful events. There is need for the application of _____a2_____psychological strategies to address life pressures to experience optimal psychological well-being and continue living meaningful and satisfactory lives. Other coping strategies are: problem-focused coping, aimed at solving the problem or changing the situation, and emotion-focused coping (e.g: avoidance, self-blame), which seeks to reduce the emotional distress associated with stressful situations.

Huang, L., Lei, W., Xu, F., Liu, H., and Yu, L. (2020). Emotional responses and coping strategies in nurses and nursing students during Covid-19 outbreak: A comparative study. *PLoS ONE* 15(8);
Panahi et al., Predictors of Psychological Well-Being among Malaysian Graduates, p. 2069.

23.

a2. _____

Gender and Coping Strategies

Research relating to emotional responses and coping strategies during the COVID-19 outbreak, involved 804 nurses (46.5%) and nursing students (53.5%), all in the 18-26 age range, while 74% was female. Nurses were problem-focused oriented more than nursing students and more women than men chose problem-focused coping when dealing with ___b2___ seeing that emotion-focused strategies were hardly a female's choice, because of their vulnerability and sensitivity to emotions.

Huang, et al. Emotional responses and coping strategies in nurses and nursing students during Covid-19 outbreak:

24.

b2. _____

Emotion- vs Problem-solving-focused Strategies

297 Iranian spouses were studied to find a link between mental health and coping styles and marital satisfaction. Findings indicate that couples who use inefficient emotion-focused strategies such as avoiding problems, they reported less marital ____c2_____. In contrast, there is a significant and positive relationship between marital adjustment and problem-focused coping strategies, in that when these were used, couples enjoy more marital satisfaction.

Reza, S. M., Ashouri, N., Akhteh, M., and Korjvandani, S. A. (2016). The Relationship between Mental Health and Coping Styles and Marital. *International Journal of Humanities and Cultural Studies*, 4, 1668-1677 (1673).

25.

c2. _____

Types of Religious Coping

Individuals find comfort, hope and spiritual guidance from religious beliefs and spiritual practices. Religion and spirituality involve coping strategies to contend with ___d2_____ , challenges, and losses. Religious coping can be positive strategies such as seeking God's love and care, and partnering with God in times of distress to find strength and relief. Negative religious coping is referred to as religious or spiritual struggles, conflict within oneself, with God, and with other people.

O'Brien, B., Shrestha, S., Stanley, M. A., Pargament, K. I., Cummings, J., Kunik, M. E., Fletcher, T. L., Cortes, J., Ramsey, D. and Amspoker, A. B. (2019). Positive and negative religious coping as predictors of distress among minority older adults. *Geriatric Psychiatry*, 34(1), 54-59 (55).

26.

d2. _____

Negative Religious Coping Strategies

Negative coping relates to an _____e2_____ relationship with God, a sense of disconnectedness with religious community, and a religious _____f2_____ in the search for meaning in life. The set of negative religious coping methods includes punitive religious reappraisals, such as perception of God's punishment for sins, spiritual discontent, in terms of feeling divinely abandoned, and self-directing religious coping (make sense of the situation without relying on God).

Lee, M., Nezu, A. M. & Nezu, C. M. (2014). Positive and negative religious coping, depressive symptoms, and quality of life in people with HIV. *Journal of Behavioral Medicine,* 37, 921–930 (922).

Positive Religious Coping and Psychological Issues I

Of the 400 Ghanaian outpatients with hypertension, 94.5% were Christians. The results revealed that the patients used spirituality to cope better emotionally, while living with a chronic condition such as hypertension. Additionally, greater spiritual well-being was associated with fewer symptoms of anxiety, depression and stress. The outcome also confirmed the _____g2_____ role of spirituality in emotional experiences that can be applicable to hypertensive patients and others with chronic conditions.

Kretchy et al., Mental health in hypertension: assessing symptoms of anxiety, depression and stress on anti-hypertensive medication adherence.

Positive Religious Coping and Psychological Issues II

Positive religious coping involves a secure relationship with God, among other ideas. The forms of positive religious coping strategies include collaborative religious coping, and seeking spiritual support. 198 individuals with HIV/AIDS, of which 60% was males, and 74% being Blacks, were studied to examine the link between religious coping and chronic disease. Positive religious coping was linked to positive outcomes such as positive affect and life ___h2___ and may contribute to ___i2___ positive, meaning-based psychological outcomes, rather than preventing negative, symptom-based ones.

Lee et al., Positive and negative religious coping, depressive symptoms, and quality of life in people with HIV, p. 928.

27.

e2. _____

f2. _____

28.

g2. _____

29.

h2. _____

i2. _____

Summary

➢ Factors which contribute to emotional difficulties can be categorized as biological, physiological, psychological, social and spiritual.

➢ Individuals need to develop resilience to be able to adapt to stressful demands and adversity in life.

➢ Chronic diseases such as cancer and NCDs such as hypertension impact negatively on our emotional health by bringing about psychological disorders such as anxiety and stress.

➢ Along with prescribed medication, various coping strategies such as adaptive responses, problem-focused strategies and positive religious coping can be used to develop resilience in order to address emotional difficulties.

a) Remember to take some time to go through the Section entitled 'A Journey Towards Total Freedom' on **pages 49-51** in *Set the Captives Free (Resource Guide).*

b) Turn to Chapters 7 and 8 to engage in this week's reading –'Comforting the Wounded' and 'Break Down' in *Raising the Wounded: Grasping for Hope in the Midst of Despair.*

Insightful Perspectives

Emotional Healthy Lifestyle Matters

Let's turn to the *emotional healthy lifestyle matters* section. These are activities and tasks we can engage in to aid our emotional, physical, psychological, relational, social and spiritual development. Some of these can be done on your own at home.

1. Building Resilience

In order to cope with various challenges, and difficulties, it is essential to develop resilience. There are four (4) main components to building resilience: connections, fostering wellness (e.g: physical activity/exercise, avoiding negativity), healthy thinking (e.g: develop balanced thinking patterns, visualize goals) and finding purpose and meaning in life (e.g: volunteering, taking initiatives to solve problems)

TASK 1

Engage in varied physical activity programme

One aspect of fostering wellness is to be physically active through engaging in different types of exercises. This aids individuals in building resilience so that we can cope with losses among other existential issues. Identify two exercises or physical activities which you have not tried as yet. Plan on implementing them over the next few days during this week. Complete the section below.

   a. The two (2) new exercises which I plan to implement are:_____
       and _____ .
   b. I plan to begin engaging in _____ (type of
       exercise) on _____ 20_____.

2. Develop an attitude of gratitude

Research shows that gratitude has significant effects on the improvement of people's mental health, it increases their well-being, strengthens their perception of social support and improves their self-esteem. Additionally, it changes resilience levels positively, increasingoptimism, and acts as a protective factor against stress and depression.

TASK 1:

   a. Write thank-you notes to individuals who has helped you along your journey.
   b. Share meaningful compliments to a friend, co-worker or colleague
   c. Celebrate the achievement or joys of someone, by hosting a toast or other appropriate activity.
   d. Identify two strengths and a skill that you possess. My strengths are:
       i)_____ and (ii)_____
       (iii)The skill I have is_____.

3. Building Relationships

It is one thing to be experiencing various emotional issues due to life's uncertain and challenging issues. However, it is another thing to be able to manage these issues. Complicated grief, financial difficulties, and unstable relationship among other struggles, require the application of effective coping strategies. It should be our desire to seek to address these and other difficulties, thereby, experiencing optimal well-being, be it on the emotional, social or spiritual level. One way to achieve this is to engage emotionally by continuing to work through the material relating to the Journey Towards Emotional Freedom which we commenced in the last Session.

TASK 1:

a) In your *Set the Captives free: 12 Studies for Individuals or Groups* Workbook, on **pages 66 – 72**, you will find activities to assist you in continuing the Journey Towards Emotional Freedom. Work through the activities on these pages as you seek to develop coping strategies for various types of emotional issues.

4. Water Intake

As part of the HEALINGS health principles on which this *Emotional Health Restoration Programme* is based, water is a key element in the **Nutrition** strand, the sixth component. Do you remember that digestion starts with saliva, whose basis is water? Digestion relies on enzymes that are found in saliva to help break down the food and liquid, after which it helps in dissolving minerals and other nutrients. Proper digestion makes minerals and nutrients more accessible to the body.

TASK 1:

CHALLENGE:

While you are attending the session today, endeavour to drink two (2) half-litre bottles of water by the end of the session. This is equivalent to four (4) cups of water.

VICTOR MARSHALL

5. Review from Previous Sessions

In the last three (3) weeks, you have taken into account various *emotional healthy lifestyle matters*, all relating to nutrition, forgiveness and emotional freedom. These areas are listed below. Please circle the answer for each activity to indicate whether or not you have been taking part in these activities. The superscript number indicates the *Session* where each lifestyle matter is found.

Engage in spiritual disciplines (Theological Reflection)[4, 5]	Doing	Not Doing
Select moody foods[4]	Doing	Not Doing
Monitor emotional eating[4]	Doing	Not Doing
Engage in spiritual disciplines (meditation/reflection)[4,5,6,7]	Doing	Not Doing
Building relationships[5,6]	Doing	Not Doing
Learning to reframe difficult emotional issues[5]	Doing	Not Doing
Reprogramme the brain[5]	Doing	Not Doing
Implement goals for relational self-care and wellness[5, 6]	Doing	Not Doing
Replace negative thoughts with inspired material[6]	Doing	Not Doing
Adequate water intake [6]	Doing	Not Doing
Practise goal-setting[6, 7]	Doing	Not Doing
Building spiritual esteem[7]	Doing	Not Doing
Paving the path for emotional freedom[7]	Doing	Not Doing

Plans & Goal Setting

On the lines below, write out **a plan for each Lifestyle activity** you need to adopt /start to practise from the list above. State the possible time of the day or of the week (e.g morning, afternoon; weekends) that you will seek to incorporate your new habits.

Alternatively, review the plans that you may have set out for yourself in Session 4 on **Page 80**. Share how you plan to begin implementing YOUR previous plans for each of the activities you marked **NOT DOING.**

Also, review the suggestions given in the **Emotional Healthy Lifestyle Section** of each previous week, as stated in this *Companion Folder*

Setting out My Plans & Goals

....

....

....

....

....

....

....

....

....

....

....

....

....

....

....

....

....

....

....

....

....

....

....

....

VICTOR MARSHALL

Personal Reflection (WEEK 8)

Reflectively Study the text below.

Prayerfully read the text below.

> Why am I discouraged?
>> Why is my heart so sad?
> I will put my hope in [*the Divine Being*]![4]
>> I will praise him again—
>> my Savior and my [*Glorious Creator*]!
>
> Now I am deeply discouraged,
>> but I will remember you—
> even from distant Mount Hermon, the source of the Jordan,
>> from the land of Mount Mizar.

_____ (Psalm 42:5-6, NLT).

a) What negative emotions are mentioned in the text?

....
....
....
....
....

b) What specific activities/actions are mentioned in the text that would bring emotional balance to your life?

....
....
....
....

- Prayerfully reflect on the verses above. Spend some time memorising the verse that appeals to you. (**WRITE *it in the space below*).**

....
....
....
....
....
....
....
....
....
....
....

- How is this text helpful to your emotional well-being?

....
....
....
....
....
....
....

- **Spend** some time praying about what the verses are saying to you. Pray also about any issues or concerns this text has raised for you about your wellbeing.

Emotional Health Lifestyle Scorecard

Week _____

ACTIVITY	DAY OF THE WEEK AND DATE						
	Sun --/--/--	**Mon** --/--/--	**Tues** --/--/--	**Wed** --/--/--	**Thurs** --/--/--	**Fri** --/--/--	**Sat** --/--/--
Spiritual Engagement * Prepare for the journey of restoration with spiritual practices (See *Set the Captives Free Workbook*, pp.15, 73							
Relationship Building Pray for a particular family member/relative/ friend with whom you are having difficulty							
Exercise Engage in Exercise. State the type and amount of time daily							
Goal-setting Identify two or three things you wish to accomplish daily AND MONTHLY. This inspires hope and optimism in that you would have accomplished a goal							
Discussion Time * Identify any two (2) issues to be addressed with a particular family member/relative/friend, and prayerfully talk to that person about the issues							
Personal Reflection How much time have you spent on the reflection activity at the end of each **SESSION**?							
Special Reading On a daily basis, read ten (10) verses from the Gospel of St Mark 1-12. Also identify and **MEMORISE** the verse that attracts you.	*Verses Read*	*Verses Read*	*Verses Read*	*Verses Read*	*Verses Read*	*Verses Read*	*Verses Read*
.... *Favourite Verse(s)*	....	....	....	....	....	....	....
Water How many glasses of water did you drink during the day?							

NOTE: * Place a tick (√) in the box next to these items to show that you have completed the activity on a daily basis. It is expected that these activities will take time and will be on-going.

NOTES

Feel free to use this space to write out the verse you are memorising from the chapter you have read this week, as a way of helping you internalise the text.

VICTOR MARSHALL

Session Nine

Improving Your Quality of Life for Emotional Health

During this session, pay attention to:

1) The two main aspects of positive mental health.

2) The impact of Non-communicable diseases on Quality of Life

3) Strategies for Improving your Quality of Life.

4) Spirituality and Quality of Life.

You will notice in your workbook that you have the outline of the PowerPoint presentation for **Session Nine**, so that you may follow along.

DVD/PowerPoint Slides

Session Nine

Improving Your Quality of Life for Emotional Health

During the PowerPoint presentations, feel free to follow along with the slides that correspond with those in the session. You can fill in the blank spaces with the missing words. Use the blanks in the margin with the letters that match to the letters on the blanks in the PowerPoint slides. (For example, for blank [a], write the answer on the line next to the section of the slide marked [a].

1.

> ## EMOTIONAL HEALTH RESTORATION PROGRAMME
>
> Identifying Emotional Dys-functionality and Possible Solutions

2.

> ## Session 9
>
> ## Improving Your Quality of Life for Emotional Health.

The Twelve 'Risk' Categories

1. Emotional Instability
2. Emotional Hurt
3. Lifestyle
4. Nutrition
5. Unforgiveness
6. Abuse
7. Unresolved Issues
8. Inability to Cope
9. **Medical Condition**
10. Childhood Adversity
11. Psychological Needs
12. Mental Functioning

Flourishing versus Languishing I

Flourishing Individuals, free of psycho-pathology such as depression and experiencing high levels of ___a___ (e.g: emotional) have ___b___ mental health. Examples of this are experiencing happiness (e.g: interested in and satisfied with life generally) and high level of positive psychological functioning (e.g: one's life has meaning,) and positive social functioning (e.g: sense of belong to a community).

Keyes, C. L. M. (2005). Mental Illness and/or Mental Health? Investigating Axioms of the Complete State Model of Health. *Journal of Consulting and Clinical Psychology*, 73(3), 539 –548 (540).

Flourishing versus Languishing II

Factors contributing to a languishing state is the absence of mental health, along with individuals never or seldom experiencing ___c___ (e.g: calmness and peace) nor positive psychological functioning in the form of personal growth (e.g: hardly experiencing personal development). Furthermore, there is very little positive social functioning, such as a lack of interest in social life.

Keyes, C. L. M. (2010). The Next Steps in the Promotion and Protection of Positive Mental Health. *Canadian Journal of Nursing Research*, 42(3), 17-28 (19-20).

3.

4.

a. _____

b. _____

5.

c. _____

Flourishing versus Languishing III

Flourishing indicates a state of _____d_____ where individuals live a satisfactory and fulfilling life. It is followed by a moderate state of mental health, which is characterized by an intermediate level of well-being and psychosocial functioning. By contrast, languishing reflects a state of _____e_____ and stagnation in which individuals are devoid of positive emotionality and meaningful engagement in life.

Chan, R. C. H., Winnie W.S. Mak, W. W. S., Chio, F. H. N. and Tong, A. C. Y. (2018). Flourishing With Psychosis: A Prospective Examination on the Interactions Between Clinical, Functional, and Personal Recovery Processes on Well-being Among Individuals with Schizophrenia Spectrum Disorders. *Schizophrenia Bulletin*, 44 (4), 778–786 (779).

6.

d. _____

e. _____

Aspects of Positive Mental Health

Positive mental health occurs along a continuum with high mental health (ie: flourishing) on one end, ____f_____ mental health being in the middle and ____g_____ mental health (ie: languishing) on the other end. Languishing indicates the absence of mental health or being mentally unhealthy. These aspects of mental health consist of emotional, psychological and social well-being, which are ___h___ to one's quality of life (QoL).

Keyes, 'The Next Steps in the Promotion and Protection of Positive Mental Health', pp.19-20.

7.

f. _____

g. _____

h. _____

Substance Misuse and Mental Health I

794 substance users (79.5% male) engaged in an Australian residential treatment programme. 69.1% had at least an upper secondary school education, but all of them struggled with the substance problem for an average of 18.28 years. The findings indicate that:
- at least 10% of the participants misused three popular substances,
- ___i___ was the most popular misused substance.

McGaffin, B. J., , Deane, F. P., Kelly, P. J. , and Ciarrochi, J. (2015). Flourishing, languishing and moderate mental health: Prevalence and change in mental health during recovery from drug and alcohol problems. *Addiction Research Theory*, 23(5), 351–360 (354, 356).

8.

i. _____

Self-reported Primary Substance Misuse

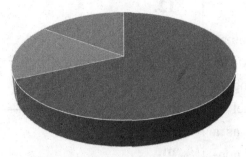

▪ Alcohol ▪ Amphetamines ▪ Cannibis

NB: The information was derived from the study conducted by McGaffin, B. J., , Deane, F. P., Kelly, P. J. , and Ciarrochi, J. (2015). Flourishing, languishing and moderate mental health: Prevalence and change in mental health during recovery from drug and alcohol problems. *Addiction Research Theory*, 23(5), 351–360 (354, 356). However, the graph was constructed b y the author of this volume.

Substance Misuse and Mental Health II

The users in this study were treated in the form of a modified therapeutic community, with 68% being single. Furthermore, the results revealed that

- more substance users were languishing during the three assessment times than those who _____j_____.

- a higher portion of those who abstained flourished in relation to users.

McGaffin, et al., Flourishing, languishing and moderate mental health: Prevalence and change in mental health during recovery from drug and alcohol problems.', pp. 354, 356.

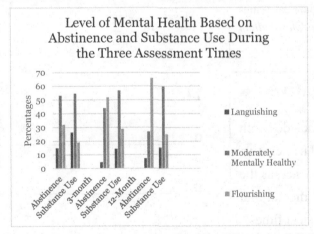

Level of Mental Health Based on Abstinence and Substance Use During the Three Assessment Times

▪ Languishing

▪ Moderately Mentally Healthy

▪ Flourishing

NB: The study was conducted by McGaffin, B. J., , Deane, F. P., Kelly, P. J. , and Ciarrochi, J. (2015). Flourishing, languishing and moderate mental health: Prevalence and change in mental health during recovery from drug and alcohol problems. *Addiction Research Theory*, 23(5), 351–360 (354, 356). However, the graph was constructed b y the author of this volume.

9.

10.

j. _____

11.

Quality of Life: What is it?

Quality of Life (QoL) covers all the aspects of human _____k_____ about the necessities of life. It also relates to individuals' _____l_____ well-being in terms of the degree of happiness or the level of _____m_____ they experience with their life as a whole. It also encompasses satisfaction about non-health-related elements such as:

- housing, employment, standard of living,
- family (e.g: marriage), interpersonal relationships (e.g: friendships),
- religion, and the environment.

12.

k. _____

l. _____

m. _____

Health-related Quality of Life: Definitions II

HRQoL is a reflection of the way that individuals perceive and react to their health _____n_____ and the non-medical aspects of their lives, which include health-related factors, such as physical, functional, emotional, and mental well-being. It also focuses on behaviours such as psychological and social functioning, along with and other situations in life.

Lin, X-J., Lin, I. and Fan, S. (2013). Methodological issues in measuring health-related quality of life. *Tzu Chi Medical Journal*, 25(1), 8-12 (8).

13.

n. _____

HRQoL: Positive vs Negative

HRQOL is a double-sided concept that includes both positive and negative aspects of health. The negative aspect includes disease and _____o_____, whereas the positive aspect encompasses feelings of mental and physical wellbeing, full functioning, physical fitness, _____p_____, and efficiency of the mind and body.

Lin, et al., 'Methodological issues in measuring health-related quality of life', p.8.

14.

o. _____

p. _____

Components of HRQoL

HRQoL also focuses on multiple components such as physical health, psychological state, level of ____q____, and social relationships, and their relationships to the important features of their environment. These are health-related, in that they are influenced by medical issues such as illness, injury, and treatment. Furthermore, it is dynamic and results from past experience, present circumstances, and expectations for the future.

Lin, et al., 'Methodological issues in measuring health-related quality of life', pp.8, 9

HRQoL and Chronic Diseases: Obesity

18,682 Spanish subjects, with about 17% being moderately to severely morbid obese (BMI > 30kg/m2) were studied. The findings indicated that the greater the ____r____ BMI, the lower participants' self-perceived health status. Also, moderate obesity and severe-to-morbid obesity greatly reduced self-perceived health status, after controlling for diagnosed chronic diseases.

Busutil, R., Espallardo, O., Torres, A., Martínez-Galdeano, L., Zozaya, N. & Hidalgo-Vega, Á. (2017). The impact of obesity on health-related quality of life in Spain. *Health Qual Life Outcomes*, 15 (197).

HRQoL and Chronic Diseases: Hypertension I

Hypertension is the leading global preventable risk factor for cardio-vascular disease and premature death. A study was conducted in a Tertiary care Hospital in India, with 300 patients over a 6- month period. 54.6% was male, while 45.3% suffered from diabetes, the most common co-morbid disease. 44.3% of the patients were aged 60+ and experienced ____s____ blood pressure more than the other age-groups. Results indicated that ___t____HRQOL in hypertensive patients was associated mainly with diabetes.

Kaliyaperumal S., Hari, S. B., Siddela, P. K. and Yadala, S. (2016). Assessment of Quality of Life in Hypertensive Patients. *Journal of Applied Pharmaceutical Science*, 6 (5), 143-147 (144).

15.

q. _____

16.

r. _____

17.

s. _____

t. _____

HRQoL and Chronic Diseases: Hypertension II

In the above-mentioned study, _____u_____ health was mostly affected in hypertensive patients followed by emotional aspects and vitality (this worsens these patients' quality of life). Low vitality indicates decreased energy due to:

- lack of ___v____ and unhealthy life styles.
- the association of hypertension with physiological and psychological symptoms (e.g: headache, anxiety) and effects of anti-hypertensive drugs (e.g: sleep disorders).

Kaliyaperumal, et al. 'Assessment of Quality of Life in Hypertensive Patients', pp.145, 146.

18.

u. _____

v. _____

HRQoL and Chronic Diseases: Stroke

Stroke is the third most prevalent cause of death globally after coronary heart disease (CHD) and cancers. It contributes to a high rate of stroke-related _____w_____, thus reducing their QoL. A study was conducted with 50 stroke survivors at the UWI Hospital in Jamaica. 42% exhibited at least mild depression, while 90% had hypertension. Results indicated that between 6 and 28 months after the stroke, the HRQOL in stroke survivors was markedly worse, with depression contributing greatly.

Pinkneya, J. A. , Gaylea, F., Mitchell-Fearon, K. and Mullings, J. (2017). Health-Related Quality of Life in Stroke Survivors at the University Hospital of the West Indies. *Journal of Neurological Research*, 7(3), 46-58 (50, 52).

19.

w. _____

Strategies for Improving Quality of Life

Health-related QoL, which measures the impact of a chronic condition on individuals' daily lives, is an essential outcome for patients living with a chronic disease. One way to improve their HRQoL is to implement ___x____ interventions (e.g: goal-setting), an approach in which patients are encouraged to take on a primary role in managing their daily care. Such interventions equip patients with essential skills to participate actively in health-enhancing behaviours so that they can manage their condition successfully.

Jonkman, N. H., Schuurmans, M. J., Groenwold, R. H. H., Hoes, A. W. and Trappenburg, J. C. A. (2016). Identifying components of self-management interventions that improve health-related quality of life in chronically ill patients: Systematic review and meta-regression analysis. In N. H. Jonkman (ed), *Self-management interventions for patients with a chronic disease: what works and in whom?* (Utretcht: University Medical Center), 42-71 (46, 47).

20.

x. _____

Strategies: Scientific Evidence

A review of 47 trials investigated the diversity of the components of self-management interventions and the impact on HRQoL. Results indicated that interventions exerted moderate positive effects on HRQoL at 6 months and 12 months follow-up. Additionally,

- interaction with peer patients impede improvement in HRQoL because of the negative link with HRQoL for T2DM patients,
- teaching patients problem-solving skills and duration of the intervention were positively associated with HRQoL in T2DM patients.

Jonkman et al., 'Identifying components of self-management interventions that improve health-related quality of life in chronically ill patients: Systematic review and meta-regression analysis'

21.

Strategies for Improving Quality of Life II

Researchers examined the health status of hypertension patients living in Chinese urban and rural areas. Of the 6 145 subjects, 2424 were urban dwellers and 3721 lived in the rural area. The results indicated that:

- physical activity (e.g: regular exercise) was a _____y_____ factor of and improved HRQoL.
- in both urban and rural areas, patients who had medical examination in the past one year had a better HRQoL

Zhang, Y., Zhou, Z., Gao, J.,Wang, D., Zhang, Q., Zhou, Z., Su, M. and Li, D. (2016). Health-related quality of life and its influencing factors for patients with hypertension: evidence from the urban and rural areas of Shaanxi Province, China. BMC Health Services Research, 16(277).

22.

y. _____

Spirituality and Quality of Life

Spiritual quality of life is individuals' perceptions of their existential well-being in the context of the culture and _____z___systems in which they live. It is also in relation to their goals, expectations, standards, and concerns. Religious practices (e.g attending religious services) have been shown to positively influence marital satisfaction, quality of life and couple functioning.

Hammer, J. H., Wade, N. G., & Cragun, R. T. (2019). Valid Assessment of Spiritual Quality of Life With the WHOQOL-SRPB BREF Across Religious, Spiritual, and Secular Persons: A Psychometric Study. *Psychology of Religion and Spirituality*, 12(4), 440-450 (440); Lister, Z., Seibert, G., Chance, S-A., Huelett, B., Wilson, L., and Wilson, C. (2020). The Influence of Prayer and Family Worship on Relationship Functioning among Married Adults in the Caribbean and Latin American. *Religions*, 11(1).

23.

z. _____

Spirituality and Quality of Life: Evidence I

3997 married Seventh-day Adventist adults in the Caribbean and Latin America, aged 18-82, has an average of 15 years of marriage. 50.5% had membership for over 10 years. More time in personal prayer and engaging in family worship more often were linked with

    i.   higher levels of relationship satisfaction,

    ii. emotional attunement in their relationships and

    iii. better conflict resolution.

This is indicative of positive relations with others and an avowed QoL, pre-requisites for positive mental health.

Lister, et al., 'The Influence of Prayer and Family Worship on Relationship Functioning among Married Adults in the Caribbean and Latin American'..

24.

Spirituality and Quality of Life: Evidence II

The data from the study of Lister et al., indicated that 49.5 % of participants were fairly new members (membership < 10 years). From the data:

    - frequent time spent studying the Sacred Word and

    - attending religious services often

led to couples reporting stronger beliefs in traditional family roles. This is indicative of couples engaging in __a2_ integration, by experiencing a sense of belonging to a community.

Lister et al., 'The Influence of Prayer and Family Worship on Relationship Functioning among Married Adults in the Caribbean and Latin American'

25.

a2._____

Divine Input and Quality of Life

The Healing Messiah and Redeemer of mankind provided an opportunity for individuals to be in good spirits, in that He has extended an invitation for individuals who are burdened, emotionally tired and ___b2____to experience rest in Him (Mt 11:28-30). On accepting this 'rest', individuals can experience positive emotional well-being in terms of displaying positive affect, whereby they can be calm and peaceful.

Bacchiocchi, S. (1984). MATTHEW 11:28-30: JESUS' REST AND THE SABBATH. *Andrews University Seminary Studies*, 22(3), 289-316 (296).

26.

b2._____

Insightful Counsel I

27.

All [*human beings*] are weighed down with burdens that only The Compassionate Saviour can remove. The heaviest burden that we bear is the burden of sin. If we were left to bear this burden, it would crush us. But the Sinless One has taken our place. "The Lord hath laid on Him the iniquity of us all" (Isaiah 53:6). He has borne the burden of our guilt. He will take the load from our weary shoulders. He will give us rest. The burden of care and sorrow also He will bear. He invites us to cast all our care upon Him; for He carries us upon His heart.

White, E. G. (1898). *The Desire of Ages* (Mountain View, CA: Pacific Press), pp.328-329.

Insightful Counsel II

28.

c2. _____

There are many whose hearts are aching under a load of care because they seek to reach the world's standard. They have chosen its service, accepted its ____c2____, [and] adopted its customs. Thus, their character is marred, and their life made a weariness. In order to gratify ambition and worldly desires, they wound the conscience, and bring upon themselves an additional burden of remorse. The continual worry is wearing out the life forces. Our Healing Creator desires them to lay aside this yoke of bondage.

White, E. G. (1898). *The Desire of Ages* (Mountain View, CA: Pacific Press), p.330

Divine Assurance and Quality of life

29.

d2. _____

Our Creator has provided an assurance that we can courageously face life's challenges since the [Evil One's]/thief's ____d2____ is to steal or take away valuable aspects of our life (e.g: peace of mind), kill and destroy us to the point that we become lost eternally. However, Our Healing Saviour's purpose is to give us a rich and satisfying life, by aiding us in experiencing a meaningful life presently and eternal life at His Second Coming.

John 10:10

Summary

➤ Individuals who have positive mental health flourish by being satisfied with life generally, live a meaningful life and have a sense of belonging to a community.

➤ Areas such as a lack of personal development and loss of purpose for living are examples of languishing, which indicates that individuals are mentally unhealthy.

➤ Health-related quality of life involves how illness, injury etc impact on one's ability to function daily and also how satisfied one is with various elements of life such as employment and relationships.

➤ Goal-setting, adoption of healthy lifestyle habits and regular medical examinations are self-management strategies used to improve one's health-related quality of life.

➤ Spiritual practices such as studying the Sacred Word and attending religious services contribute to the improvement of one's spiritual quality of life.

Insightful Perspectives

a) Remember to take some time to go through the Section entitled 'A Biblical Perspective of Restoration' on **pages 6-7** in *Set the Captives Free: Experiencing Healing Through Holistic Restoration (Resource Guide).*

b) Turn to Chapter 9 and engage in the week's reading –'The Trip that Turn the Tide in *Raising the Wounded: Grasping for Hope in the Midst of Despair.*

Emotional Healthy Lifestyle Matters

Let's turn to the *emotional healthy lifestyle matters* section. These are activities and tasks we can engage in to aid our emotional, physical, psychological, relational, social and spiritual development. Some of these can be done on your own at home.

1. Building Relationships

Healthy and positive interpersonal relationships require a display of wholesome attitudes and behaviours and healthy interactions with others. In **Sessions 5 to 8,** we embarked on building relationships by focusing on forgiveness and emotional freedom. In this

Session, it is important to apply the various biblical principles which we encountered while addressing these emotional issues. Another way is to achieve harmony by rebuilding broken relationship bridges. The material relating to the Journey Towards Reconciliation is useful for this objective.

TASK 1:

a) In your *Set the Captives free: 12 Studies for Individuals or Groups* Workbook, on **pages 76 – 78**, you will find activities to assist you in beginning the Journey Towards Reconciliation. Work through the activities on these pages as you seek to begin your journey.

2. Adequate Water Intake

Coconut water is a very beneficial option to plain water, in that, from a nutritional perspective, it is helps us to stay hydrated while it is low in calories and free of fats and cholesterol. Additionally, it is high in micro-nutrients such as magnesium, potassium and sodium in an effort to aid in the replenishing of any lost nutrients. It aids in the elimination of waste such as extra chloride and sodium from your body through your urine. Furthermore, coconut water helps to lower blood pressure. However, hypertensive individuals using medication should consult their medical team prior to using this valuable type of water.

This tropical beverage is also a traditional medicine, a microbiological growth medium and is a useful rehydrating and refreshing drink after physical exercise.

Source: Prades et al. (2012). Coconut water uses, composition and properties: a review. *Fruits*, 62(7), 78-107.

TASK 1:

Prepare to increase you water intake **TODAY** during the programme. Bring along two (2) half-litre bottles of coconut water so that you can be refreshed and be hydrated.

3. Maintain Your Physical Activity Programme

Most lifestyle changes become a routine with time, thereby making an impact so that you can experience the benefits. This section requires you to provide an update on your exercise routine so that you can gauge *your progress* in this lifestyle habit.

    a.   What types of physical activities have you been engaged in for at least 30 mins per day for at least five days a week?

    _____

    b.   If you have been involved in at least three (3) different types, then continue on your programme. You are doing remarkably well.

    c.   If you have been involved in **less than two** (2) different types of physical activities, select two (2) other activities which you are willing to undertake over the next week. **R**eview the possible choices in SESSION ONE's Lifestyle Matters on **Page 13** in this *Companion Folder.* **SELECT THE TWO** which you **WILL** do this week.

SHARE them here: (i)_____ ii)_____

4. Assessment

Genograms are useful tools which clinicians use to gather information about a person's family of orientation (e.g: parents, relatives, siblings) and family of procreation (e.g: nuclear/ single-parent family). It provides a detailed pictorial display of family dynamics in relation to emotional and social relationships.

<u>TASK 1:</u>

Turn to the **Blank Sheet** with the diagram for your **Genogram** and complete it as best as you can. Attempt to complete each level which represents each generation, by beginning with yourself at the bottom of the sheet.

Personal Reflection (WEEK 9)

Reflectively Study the text below.

> Be still in the presence of the ALMIGHTY,
>> and wait patiently for him to act.
> Don't worry about evil people who prosper
>> or fret about their wicked schemes.
> [8] Stop being angry!
>> Turn from your rage!
> Do not lose your temper—
>> it only leads to harm.
>
> _____(Psalm 37:7-8, NLT).

- Which of the verses attracted you attention? *(Write it out in the space below)*

....

....

....

....

....

....

....

....

....

....

....

....

....

....

- Identify any **two (2)** emotions mentioned in the text that can negatively impact on your quality of life. Briefly describe how they can impact on you.

....
....
....
....
....
....
....

- Write down any insights you have gained from these verses above.

....
....
....
....
....
....
....

- What can you do to follow the guidance in the verses mentioned above in order to experience better mental health?

....
....
....
....
....
....

After having read these verses, what impact did they have on you?

....

....

....

....

....

....

....

....

....

....

....

• What steps would you need to take in order to gain a positive transformation in your life over the next few weeks?

....

....

....

....

....

....

....

....

....

....

....

Emotional Health Lifestyle Scorecard

Week _____

ACTIVITY	DAY OF THE WEEK AND DATE						
	Sun ----/----/----	Mon ----/----/----	Tues ----/----/----	Wed ----/----/----	Thurs ----/----/----	Fri ----/----/----	Sat ----/----/----
Spiritual Engagement * Prepare for the journey of restoration with spiritual practices (*See the Captives Free Workbook*, pp.15, 73							
Relationship Building Pray for a particular family member/relative/ friend with whom you are having difficulty							
Exercise Engage in Exercise. State the type and amount of time daily							
Goal-setting Identify two or three things you wish to accomplish daily AND MONTHLY. This inspires hope and optimism in that you would have accomplished a goal							
Discussion Time * Identify any two (2) issues to be addressed with a particular family member/relative/friend, and prayerfully talk to that person about the issues							
Personal Reflection How much time have you spent on the reflection activity at the end of each **SESSION**?							
Special Reading On a daily basis, read ten (10) verses from the Gospel of St Mark 1-12. Also identify and **MEMORISE** the verse that attracts you. .... *Favourite Verse(s)*	*Verses Read*	*Verses Read*	*Verses Read*	*Verses Read*	*Verses Read*	*Verses Read*	*Verses Read*
Water How many glasses of water did you drink during the day?							

NOTE: * Place a tick (√) in the box next to these items to show that you have completed the activity on a daily basis. It is expected that these activities will take time and will be on-going.

VICTOR MARSHALL

NOTES

Feel free to use this space to write out the verse you are memorising from the chapter you have read this week, as a way of helping you internalise the text.

Session Ten
Rising Beyond Childhood Adversity

During this session, pay attention to:

1) Theoretical perspectives of development during early childhood.

2) Types of adverse childhood experiences (ACEs).

3) The impact of ACEs on the human body such as the brain and the immune system.

4) The connection between social and psychological dysfunction and ACEs.

5) Interventions which can counteract the negative effects of ACEs.

You will notice in your workbook that you have the outline of the PowerPoint presentation for **Session Ten**, so that you may follow along.

DVD/PowerPoint Slides

Session Ten

Rising Beyond Childhood Adversity

During the PowerPoint presentations, feel free to follow along with the slides that correspond with those in the session. You can fill in the blank spaces with the missing words. Use the blanks in the margin with the letters that match to the letters on the blanks in the PowerPoint slides. (For example, for blank [a], write the answer on the line next to the section of the slide marked [a].

1.

> ## EMOTIONAL HEALTH RESTORATION PROGRAMME
>
> Identifying Emotional Dys-functionality and Possible Solutions

2.

> ## Session 10
>
> Rising Beyond Childhood Adversity

Early Childhood Age Range

Researchers have embraced the view that early childhood encompasses the age span from birth to six years. This group of children are heavily ____a_____ on significant others (e.g: parents) and there are similarities between biological and cognitive _____b_____. Additionally, this area of human development consists of unique developmental traits which are different from those which emerge after age 8.

Stephen, C. (2010). Pedagogy: the silent partner in early years learning. *Early Years: An International Journal of Research and Development*, 30(1), 15-28 (15); Gullo, D. F. (2005). *Understanding Assessment and Evaluation in Early Childhood Education* (NY: Teachers' College Press), p.5

3.

a. _____

b. _____

Developmental Stages of Early Childhood

Early childhood ages are represented by the oral (0-18 months), anal (18 months -3 years) and phallic (3 – 6 years) stages of __c____ development based on Freud's (1964) theory. Erikson's (1982) perspective of human development indicates that early childhood span over three stages: infancy (0 – 1.5 years), early childhood (1.5 – 3 years) and play years (3 -6 years).

Batra, S. (2013). The Psychosocial Development of Children: Implications for Education and Society — Erik Erikson in Context. *Contemporary Education Dialogue*, 10(2), 249–278 (258). Gullo, '*Understanding Assessment and Evaluation in Early Childhood Education*', p.5.

4.

c. _____

Developmental Perspectives: Freud I

Freud 's developmental stages span birth through puberty and incorporates psycho-sexual concepts which explain ____d____ development. During each stage, individuals experience tension and anxiety which must be managed, seeing that many of the individual differences in adult personality emerge because of a failure to progress from one stage of development to the next. This lack of development leads to _____e___. Trauma or emotional stress may also lead to a partial _____f___ to an earlier stage's behaviours.

Hayslip, B., Jr., Neumann, C. S., Louden, L., & Chapman, B. (2006). Developmental Stage Theories. In J. C. Thomas, D. L. Segal, & M. Hersen (Eds.), *Comprehensive Handbook of Personality and Psychopathology, Vol. I. Personality and Everyday Functioning* (NJ: John Wiley & Sons Inc), pp. 115–141(116).

5.

d. _____

e. _____

f. _____

Developmental Perspectives: Freud II

The oral stage includes tasks such as biting, chewing and sucking which give sexual _____g_____. Disruption in instant gratification of oral needs results in an imbalance between frustration and gratification, thus the child becomes ____h____. At the anal stage, toilet training illustrates the delicate developmental task of balancing personal gratification needs with society's expectations. At this stage, the toddler is aided in developing the ego and self-control. Too much pressure can lead to disorganization, obsessive _____i_____ and/or stubbornness.

Hayslip, 'Developmental Stage Theories', pp. 116, 117.

6.

g. _____

h. _____

i. _____

Developmental Perspectives: Freud III

Children at phallic stage focus their libidinal energy on the opposite-sex parent. For boys, this is labelled the Oedipus complex, while in girls, it is called the Electra complex. The male child's sexual energy is directed toward the mother and the girl's desire is directed toward her father. Resolving this dilemma is by way of _____j_____ with the same-sex parent, while ____k____ the desire for the opposite-sex parent and the hostility toward the same-sex parent. As a result, the superego and gender-appropriate interests and actions are developed.

Hayslip, Developmental Stage Theories., p. 117

7.

j. _____

k. _____

Developmental Perspectives: Erik Erikson I

Erikson's psycho-social perspective indicate that social aspects (e.g: interactions) which __l__ human development are important in shaping the identity of human personality. Erikson's views have major implications for practitioners such as child psychologists, counsellors, educators and health psychologists. They are required to assess developmental __m__ or lack thereof, and recommend appropriate interventions and treatments.

Batra, 'The Psychosocial Development of Children', p. 250.

8.

l. _____

m. _____

Developmental Perspectives: Erik Erikson II

In the early months, an infant, in a loving and secured home, lives with being trusted and learns to trust others, which inspired ____n____ as a virtue. Being deprived of care and reliable love create mistrust, leading to ____o____, a pathological behaviour. Toddlers desire to experience autonomy should be aided through sensitive parental guidance. The basic virtue that emerges is a sense of will to make choices that are relevant for the present and subsequent ages. When they are hindered, a sense of doubt and shame emerges.

Batra, 'The Psychosocial Development of Children', pp. 257, 259.

Developmental Perspectives: Erik Erikson III

According to Erikson, successful passage through previous stages aid children's engagement in fantasy and play. These activities are seen as taking ____p____ to fulfil an important developmental need for social exchange and problem solving relevant to their age. These experiences enable them to develop a sense of purpose. When they are denied the psychological, physical and social space necessary for developing this quality, children develop negative emotions namely self-doubt and guilt. They become enraged with self and others, and instead develop a sense of inhibition.

Batra, 'The Psychosocial Development of Children', p. 262.

The Impact of Trauma on the Body I

The brain and the immune system are not fully formed at birth. Experiences in early phases of postnatal development, contribute to the brain and the immune system progressively expanding *to* maximize ____q____ to stimuli that are specific to the individual's environment. Childhood psychosocial stressors (e.g: parental divorce) tend to affect the development of the immune system which in turn can affect brain development and its long-term functioning.

Danese, A. and Lewis, S. J. (2017). Psychoneuroimmunology of Early-Life Stress: The Hidden Wounds of Childhood Trauma? *Neuropsychopharmacology Reviews*, 42: 99-114 (99).

9.

n. _____

o. _____

10.

p. _____

11.

q. _____

Insightful Guidelines I

The impressions made on the heart early in life are seen in after years. They may be ___r___, but they will seldom be obliterated. The first three years is the time in which to bend the tiny *[child]*. Mothers should understand the importance attaching to this period. It is then that the ___s_____ is laid. If these first lessons have been defective, as they very often are, for Christ's sake, for the sake of your children's future and eternal good, seek to repair the wrong you have done.

White, E. G. (1923). *Child Guidance* (Washington, D.C.: Review and Herald Publishing Association), p. 194.

12.

r. _____

s. _____

Insightful Guidelines II

The lessons that the child learns during the first seven years of life have more to do with forming his ___t___ than all that it learns in future years. ... Virtues are to be instilled into his opening mind. The parents' work must begin with the child in its infancy, that it may receive the right impress of character ere the world shall place its stamp on mind and heart. It is during the first years of a child's life that his __u___ is most susceptible to impressions either good or evil. During these years decided progress is made in either a right direction or a wrong one.

White, *Child Guidance*, p.193

13.

t. _____

u. _____

The Twelve 'Risk' Categories

1. Emotional Instability
2. Emotional Hurt
3. Lifestyle
4. Nutrition
5. Unforgiveness
6. Abuse
7. Unresolved Issues
8. Inability to Cope
9. Medical Condition
10. **Childhood Adversity**
11. Psychological Needs
12. Mental Functioning

14.

Adverse Childhood Experiences (ACEs)

Traumatic events occurring during childhood are adverse childhood experiences. They produce toxic stress which is a prolonged activation of the stress response. The features are:

- the body fails to ___v___ fully or function properly
- a lack of caregiver ___w___ reassurance, or emotional attachments.
- Low caretaker support prevents the buffering of the stress response.

Franke, H. A. (2014). Toxic Stress: Effects, Prevention and Treatment. *Children.* 1(3):390-402. (392).

15.

v. _____

w. _____

Adverse Childhood Experiences (ACEs)

The adverse childhood experiences can be categorised as:

- abuses (e.g: emotional, physical, sexual)
- ___x___ dysfunctionality (e.g: criminality, divorce, domestic violence, substance abuse)
- psychological (e.g: mental illness)
- ___y___ (extreme poverty, low socio-economic status, neglect).

Oral, R., Ramirez, M., Coohey, C., Nakada, S., Walz, A., Kuntz, A., Benoit, J. & Peek-Asa Adverse childhood experiences and trauma informed care: the future of health care. *Pediatric Research*, 79 (1), 227–233 (227).

16.

x. _____

y. _____

ACEs and Physiological Stress Response I

Stress response activates the hypothalamic–pituitary–adrenal (HPA) axis and the sympathetic nervous system which respond to stressors. The activation begins in the brain's hypothalamus with the release of ___z___, which then stimulates the release of a hormone from the anterior pituitary, and leads to the release of stress hormones (e.g: cortisol) from the adrenal cortex. When the HPA axis is activated and cortisol is released, a negative feedback loop keeps the stress response from becoming ___a2___. Apart from the loop, the elimination of the environmental stressor helps the spike in stress hormones return to baseline quickly and easily.

Oral, et al., 'Adverse childhood experiences and trauma informed care:', pp. 227-228.

17.

z. _____

a2. _____

Impact of ACEs on Immune System

Recent reviews of studies found that cumulative exposure to childhood maltreatment such as abuses (e.g: physical, sexual) was associated with ___b2____ in plasma inflammation levels, resulting in low white blood cell count and low fibrinogen, the protein in blood plasma. Such childhood traumatic events (e.g: peer bullying) cause an inflammatory immune system, with the effects reaching into _____c2_____.

Baumeister, D., Akhtar, R., Ciufolini, S., Pariante, C. M.1 and Mondelli, V. (2016). Childhood trauma and adulthood inflammation: a meta-analysis of peripheral C-reactive protein, interleukin-6 and tumour necrosis factor-α. *Molecular Psychiatry,*21, 642–649 (647); Danese and Lewis, 'Psychoneuroimmunology of Early-Life Stress ', pp.102-103.

18.

b2._____

c2._____

Impact of ACEs on Brain Development

The toxic consequences of stress on brain function and mental and physical health is evident. One of the mechanisms through which _____d2_____affects the health and well-being of children and adults is via the toxic effects of stress on the _____e2_____. Poverty tends to affect physiologic and neuro-biological development of children.

Blair, C. and Raver, C. (2016). Poverty, Stress, and Brain Development: New Directions for Prevention and Intervention. *Academic Pediatrics,*16(3), pp. S30-S36 (S31).

19.

d2._____

e2._____

Research Evidence

A study involved the analysis of magnetic images of 389 children, aged 4 to 22 years, whose families had an average of 5 members, with 25% of the households being poor. Findings indicate that family poverty had reduced children's gray matter volumes in the brain's frontal and temporal cortex and the hippocampus. An increase in poverty levels for families was associated with a decrease in gray matter of the brain.

Hair, N. L., Hanson, J. L., Wolfe, B. L., and Pollak, S. D. (2015). Association of Child Poverty, Brain Development, and Academic Achievement. *JAMA Pediatrics,* 169 (9), pp.822–829.

20.

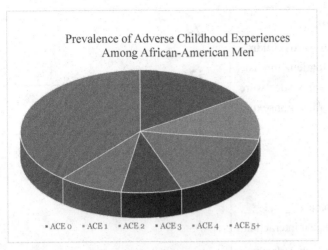

Prevalence of Adverse Childhood Experiences Among African-American Men

■ ACE 0   ■ ACE 1   ■ ACE 2   ■ ACE 3   ■ ACE 4   ■ ACE 5+

NB: The study was conducted by Topitzes, J., Pate, D. J., Berman, N. D., & Medina-Kirchner, C. (2016). Adverse childhood experiences, health, and employment: A study of men seeking job services. *Child Abuse & Neglect*, 61, pp. 23–34 (28,29,30). However, the graph was constructed b y the author of this volume.

21.

Social Dysfunctionality

199 men (94.5% African American), aged 16 to 63, experienced ACEs. 12.6% was married or partnered and 76.8% single. 45.0 % has a high school diploma, 8.5% earned a degree and 75 %+ had a low yearly income (≤ $10,000). Results reveal that Black men seeking ___**f2**___ services:

i.   were exposed to __**g2**_ rates of specific childhood adversities
ii. suffered from more accumulated childhood adversities
iii. experienced five or more adverse situations (almost 40%)

Topitzes, J., Pate, D. J., Berman, N. D., & Medina-Kirchner, C. (2016). Adverse childhood experiences, health, and employment: A study of men seeking job services. *Child Abuse & Neglect,* 61, pp. 23–34 (28,29,30).

22.

f2._____

g2._____

ACEs and Social Dysfunctionality

In the Topitzes et al study above, 63% of the participants had at least one child, 35% completed postsecondary education without qualifications and 2.5% earned from $30,000 to $50,000 yearly. Findings also revealed that Black men seeking job services who were exposed to 5+ ACEs:

a. had a history of ___**h2**____ problems (68.8%).
b. currently smoked (66.2%) and
c. were arrested or incarcerated (65.8%).

Topitzes, et al., 'Adverse childhood experiences, health, and employment', pp.28, 29.

23.

h2._____

ACEs and Social Deficits

66 male sex offenders (average age 47 years) towards children and adults were recruited from a Dutch inpatient forensic psychiatric hospital for a study. The following issues were more prevalent for child sexual offenders than nonsexual violent offenders in this study:

- _____i2_____
- shame
- Social isolation

Incompetent parenting results in children's insecure ____j2____, thus contributing to social deficits and negative peer interaction.

Chakhssi, F., de Ruiter, C., & Bernstein, D. P. (2013). Early Maladaptive Cognitive Schemas in Child Sexual Offenders Compared with Sexual Offenders against Adults and Nonsexual Violent Offenders: An Exploratory Study. The Journal of Sexual Medicine, 10(9), 2201–2210.

Impact of ACEs: Psychosis

A study involved 1825 Australians (60 % male), age ranges (18–34 years and 35–65 years) and 58% had a mental history. Data indicate

- 80% of Australians living with psychosis experienced at least one ACE
- 87% was ____k2_____, 68 % experienced non-affective psychosis and
- 16.6 % reported exposure to ACE on at least one occasion before 18 years of age

Turner S, Harvey C, Hayes L, Castle D, Galletly C, Sweeney S, Shah S, Keogh L, Spittal MJ (2020). Childhood adversity and clinical and psychosocial outcomes in psychosis. *Epidemiology and Psychiatric Sciences* 29, e78, 1–10.

Impact of ACEs: Substance Abuse and Distress

242 African-American children (51.2 % females) were studied for 35 years, from ages 6 to 42 years. Findings indicate that

- __l2__ socio-economic status in early years for females positively affected psychological distress in early adulthood.
- Poor maternal mental health increased risk for low school ___m2___ in females which led to adult drug use.
- Males with a low childhood SES increased the risk of ___n2__ health problems in adolescence.

Fothergill K, Ensminger ME, Doherty EE, Juon H-S, Green KM. Pathways from Early Childhood Adversity to Later Adult Drug Use and Psychological Distress: A Prospective Study of a Cohort of African Americans. *Journal of Health and Social Behavior.* 2016;57(2):223-239 (232, 233).

24.

i2. _____

j2. _____

25.

k2. _____

26.

l2. _____

m2. _____

n2. _____

Impact of ACEs: hypertension

Exposure to ACEs disrupts the ___**o2**____ of the immune system, thus creating a risk for heart-related disease. A review of 40 studies involving the impact of ACEs on physical health, indicates that of the 13 studies assessing BP and/or hypertension only, 8 studies identified:

- a positive link between child maltreatment and hypertension.
- an association between hypertension varied based on the type or ____**p2**_____ of maltreatment.

Basu, A., McLaughlin, K. A., Misra, S., & Koenen, K. C. (2017). Childhood maltreatment and health impact: The examples of cardiovascular disease and type 2 diabetes mellitus in adults. *Clinical Psychology: Science and Practice, 24*(2), 125–139.

27.

o2._____

p2._____

Offset ACEs: Interventions in Adulthood

Social support, an adaptive coping strategy, relates to social networks (e.g. number of contacts), and enacted support, (ie gaining practical and emotional assistance). These practical elements eliminate social isolation, which can lead to withdrawal, a maladaptive coping strategy. In a study, involving 202 British participants with psychosis, aged 16-64, findings indicate that a lack of support in adulthood was associated with increased odds of psychosis in women who reported childhood physical abuse.

Gayer-Anderson, C., Fisher, H.L., Fearon, P. *et al.* (2015). Gender differences in the association between childhood physical and sexual abuse, social support and psychosis. *Social Psychiatry and Psychiatric Epidemiology,* 50, **pp.**1489–1500 (1490).

28.

_q2____ Resilience Positively Impacts on ACEs

Early life circumstances cannot be altered in old age. However, resilience is ____**r2**_____ and can be fostered throughout life using various strategies. Building resilience, in relation to self-rated health is advantageous for identifying and strengthening the personal assets and environmental resources and, therefore, seem to preserve self-related health. From a study of 1506 individuals, aged 65-74, findings indicate that resilience can build the ___**s2**___ and biological strengths to improve self-related health among older adults and minimise the harms of early economic hardship.

Lau, S. Y. Z., Guerra, R. O., Barbosa, J. F. dS., & Phillips, S. P. (2018). Impact of resilience on health in older adults: a cross-sectional analysis from the International Mobility in Aging Study (IMIAS). BMJ Open, 8.

29.

q2._____

r2._____

s2._____

Detoxification Diet and Toxins

Sustained stress from adverse difficulties can produce chronic high levels of cortisol (stress hormone), leading to ___t2___ stress. This type of stress contributes to poor health outcomes (e.g: obesity). Additionally, metals such as lead and mercury can deposit toxins in the body. Detoxification diets are short-term interventions designed to eliminate toxins from the body and promote health. Foods such as fruits, raw vegetables, water, citric acid and Chlorella (a type of green algae) are useful for eliminating the toxins.

Klein, A. V., & Kiat, H. (2014). Detox diets for toxin elimination and weight management: a critical review of the evidence. *Journal of Human Nutrition and Dietetics*, 28(6), pp.675-686

30.

t2. _____

Impact of Spirituality on ACEs

Research with 7554 individuals (91.4% Caucasians), 67.6% being married and most (33.4%) in the 29-39 age group, indicates that 63 % associated spirituality (e.g: meditation, purposeful life) with helping them to navigate difficult life____u2___. Results revealed that they:

- experienced better life outcomes (relationships and resilience
- reframed their early hardships into divine purposes,
- counteracted the __v2____ effects of childhood adversity, and experienced feelings of dignity and worth.

Woods, S. H., Allen, K. M., & Larwin, K. H. (2020). How We Rise: Overcoming Trauma with Healthy Life Outcomes and Spiritual Counsel. *Journal of Mental Health and Social Behaviour*, 2(1):

31.

u2._____

v2._____

Massage Therapy for Anxiety

Massage therapy increases blood flow in arteries and veins and increases the ___w2____ and dopamine, while decreasing cortisol levels. Additionally, it stimulates the central nerve system and decrease the heart rate and respiration. In a study with 50 heart failure patients, whose average age was 69.13 years, findings revealed that:

- females reported higher levels of test anxiety than males.
- males showed greater reduction in anxiety than the females
- massage therapy ___x2_ anxiety in patients admitted to ICU.

Ramezanli, S., Jahromi, M. K., Talebizadeh, M., and Poorgholami, F. (2016). Measuring the Effect of Massage Therapy on Anxiety of Heart Failure Patients. *Bioscience Biotechnology Research Asia*, 13(1), pp. 435-439 (437).

32.

w2. _____

x2._____

Summary

➢ Early childhood experiences negatively impact on children psycho-sexual and psycho-social development,

➢ Children under 18 years of age, living in poverty-stricken homes tend to experience issues such as abuse, neglect, and unstable homes. These experiences have led to various types of healthy issues such as heart diseases, and obesity.

➢ Social dysfunctionality indicates that a social skills and performance deficit exist where there is a lack of skills to engage in social interaction and inadequate performance because of factors such as anxiety.

➢ Detox diets, spirituality and massage therapy are some of the interventions which can offset the toxic stress generated from adverse childhood experiences.

> **a)** Remember to take some time to go through the Section entitled 'Social Restoration on **Page 23** in *Set the Captives Free (Resource Guide).*
>
> **b)**Turn to Chapter 10 and engage in the week's reading –'The Intruder' in *Raising the Wounded: Grasping for Hope in the Midst of Despair.*

Insightful Perspectives

Emotional Healthy Lifestyle Matters

Let's turn to the *emotional healthy lifestyle matters* section. These are activities and tasks we can engage in as a means of aiding our emotional, intellectual physical, psychological, relational, social and spiritual development. Some of these can be done on your own at home.

1. Breath of Fresh Air

Research studies indicate that stress contribute to mental health issues such as anxiety and depression. However, there can be negative effects on you physically, and this includes the suppression of your immune system, thereby resulting in you becoming sick more than usual.

One healthy and simple way to manage stress is practise deep breathing. This technique allows you to inhale air through your nose fully which would fill your lungs. Consequently, it helps to slow your heart rate and lower or stabilize your blood pressure.

For instance, research reveals that an increase supply of oxygen sent to your brain, can stimulate your parasympathetic nervous system, thus, promoting a state of serenity. Regularly practicing breathing techniques can help you block your awareness of your worries racing through your mind.

Starting TODAY, let's engage in deep breathing. With correct posture, erect standing or sitting, spend the next 5 minutes taking deep breath. Prepare to spend about 20 minutes per day doing this for 3 days. This will eventually result in you doing about 4 sessions of the activity.

2. 'Flush' the Mind through Wholesome Activities

'Flushing' the mind gives you the opportunity to address some of the negativity which has emerged from you past experiences. Adverse childhood experiences tend to create mental anguish from various traumatic situations. One way to reset the mind to the original pathway is to memorise wholesome material in order to re-channel the thoughts, and by extension, heal the mind. This activity aids you in creating a conducive and positive internal **Environment,** the second component of the HEALINGS health principles. Importantly, this is beneficial for ensuring that your emotional environment is void of negative emotions such as anger and tension.

TASK 1

a) Prayerfully, read the following text aloud and slowly:

> *I have told you these things, so that in Me you may have [perfect] peace. In the world you have tribulation and distress and suffering, but be courageous [be confident, be undaunted, be filled with joy]; I have overcome the world."* *[My conquest is accomplished, My victory abiding.]* John 16:33, AMP.

b) **Re-write** the text on the lines below and memorize it twice daily during this week.

....

....

....

....

....
....
....
....
....

c) What insights or message have you gained from reflecting on this text?

....
....
....
....
....
....
....
....

3. Detox Diet

Various reasons have been cited for engaging in detox therapy. Some of these are environmental exposure to toxins (e.g: lead,), general cleansing/preventative medicine, gastrointestinal disorders, auto-immune disease, inflammation, chronic fatigue syndrome, stress release and weight loss. Importantly, the body eliminates unwanted substances through the natural detoxifiers: digestive and lymphatic systems, kidneys, liver, lungs, and skin. However, adverse childhood experiences have created toxic stress in our bodies, resulting in numerous health challenges. Therefore, a manual detox gives the human body a boost in order to cope with the sustained toxic stress.

A detox allows you to reinforce the principles on nutrition which you encountered in Session 4, **Page 67**. Additionally, a diet rich in vitamins and minerals, with plenty of fruits and vegetables and which avoids alcohol, caffeine and tobacco will improve the condition of your hair, nails and skin.

Nutrient-rich foods with phyto-chemicals and anti-oxidants, enable the body to cope with stress and allow you to feel calmer, thereby, allowing you to concentrate and think clearly.

SOURCE: Pannell, M. (2009). *The Detox Health-plan Cookbook* (St. Helens: The Book People Ltd), p.20.

Detox Challenge

In starting out on a detox programme, it is advisable to begin with a weekend so that you can adjust to a long programme if you so desire (e.g: one- or two-week plan). The *weekend detox programme* is a strict regime which features fruits, juices, vegetable dishes, and water for only two days. One benefit is that it gives your digestive system a rest, allowing the body to eliminate any stored toxins and recuperate from stress overload.

Detox Programme Guidelines

It consists of three 'meals' per day: breakfast, lunch and dinner. Plenty of water is necessary, along with vitamin-rich juices and herbal teas.

i.   Choose a weekend when you are free to rest and relax completely, without distractions or pressure to fulfil an appointment.

ii.   Reduce your intake of normal foods at least a week in advance to allow the body to adjust and to prevent withdrawal symptoms due to the reduction of addictive foods.

iii.   If you are unwell and are taking medication for any health issue, consult with your family doctor first.

iv.   Individuals under age 18 and over 65 should consult with family members, rather than embark on the detox programme alone.

v.   Put away foods which are not included in the detox menu and remove any kitchen appliance which you do not need for the weekend.

vi.   Acquire, airtight containers to carry lunchtime food to work, steamer for cooking vegetables, and a water-filter.

vii.   Prepare your bathroom to give yourself a calm and relaxing environment and stock up with the needed items (e.g: face scrub).

viii.   Set the mood by (a) tidying up the house, allow fresh air, having relaxing Gospel music/instrumentals and reading materials.

ix.   Light up your environment with light shades of blue for a calming and relaxing time; pale green to make you feel cooler and comfortable.

x.   Prepare to include engage in 15-20 minute walks at least three times a week, if you have not started.

TAKE SOME TIME TO ENSURE THAT YOU ARE READY FOR YOUR WEEKEND BY REVIEWING THE GUIDELINES ABOVE

MEAL PLANS [Consult your vegetarian cook book]

Friday:

Dinner: (a)Vegetable/pumpkin soup; or steam vegetables with lentil soup; or steam broccoli with sesame seeds; with mixed green leaf and herb salad

RELAX after a warm shower/bath.

Meditate on **Psalm 121** and journal insights

Sabbath/Saturday

Morning: Do your devotions along with a cup of warm water with some lemon juice.

Stimulate the lymphatic system with some simple stretches. Take a dry skin brush to stimulate the circulation system, then take a warm shower or bath.

Breakfast: Fragrant fruit salad/apple fruit salad or smoothie; herbal tea.

Attend worship service

Lunch: Chilled tomato or vegetable juice or alternative juice; large Greek salad with light herbal dressing (extra virgin oil, basal, garlic etc). Alternatively, prepare carrot/pumpkin soup; red pepper and sprout salad with cashew cream dressing; OR beans and vegetables soup and basic tossed green salad. Include your nuts and grains

Afternoon: Take a short rest; relax and read or journal with instrumental music/ attend church service; refreshing juice, water

Resume your meditation on **Psalm 121** and continue to journal insights

Dinner: Lightly cooked vegetable dish; steamed broccoli with carrot and raisin Salad. Cinnamon and butternut squash smoothie

Evening: RELAX after a warm shower or bath. Choose calming music and a cup of peppermint or chamomile tea.

REVIEW YOUR WEEKEND SO FAR AND GAUGE HOW WELL YOU HAVE BEEN ON TRACK WITH THE PROGRAMME

Sunday:

Take your time seeing that you may be feeling tired or cold. The body could be experiencing a 'cleansing crisis' which is when stored toxins are released into the system to be flushed out.

REPEAT THE SAME ROUTINE AS WAS DONE ON SABBATH/SATURDAY

➢ Choose different fruit and vegetable juices; fruit salads (mango, melon, bananas)
➢ Select different soups (e.g: Brussels sprout, mushroom, split peas chowder; kidney beans soup)
➢ A variety of salads (Asian cucumber salad, with sesame seeds, and red onion; citrus walnut tossed salad)
➢ Complete your meditation on **Psalm 121** and journal insights
➢ RELAX with a warm shower or bath

4. Massage Therapy

Complementary therapies have become increasingly essential in wholistic health and therapeutic programmes. Some of these are hydrotherapy, massage therapy and meditation.

Massage therapy (MT) is a technique that promotes the manual mobilization of muscles and tissue, by applying mechanical force to those areas. MT can provide physiological and psychological benefits such as stimulating the lymphatic system to reduce fluid retention, promoting a general state of happiness and reducing bodily tension.

TASK 1

To improve lymphatic drainage to the feet and legs, try a **daily skin 'brush'** using your finger-tips.

i. Begin by working on the thighs. This cleanses the lymphatic channels in this region so that it is ready to receive the lymph foods from the lower legs.
ii. Briskly brush all over the thigh from knee to its top, three or four times **DAILY.**
iii. Work on the lower legs in a similar way. Brush either side of the leg from ankle to knee, then treat the back of the leg. Follow this by brushing along the top of the leg to the knee.
iv. Brush over each area twice more, making it three times in total.

5. Building Relationships

Healthy and positive interpersonal relationships require a display of wholesome attitudes and behaviours and healthy interactions with others. In **Session 9,** we embarked on seeking to achieve harmony by rebuilding broken relationship bridges. In this **Session,** it is important to continue applying the various biblical principles which we have encountered while addressing these emotional issues. The material relating to the Journey Towards Reconciliation is useful for this objective.

TASK 1:

a) In your *Set the Captives free: 12 Studies for Individuals or Groups* Workbook, on **pages 79 – 81**, you will find activities to assist you in continuing on the Journey Towards Reconciliation. Work through the activities on these pages as you continue on your journey.

6. Assessment

Having begun working on your genogram, you would have noticed that it allowed you to track your family history and provides information about your genealogy, and the different types of family relationships through a lineage. Furthermore, the genogram aids us in identifying family members' and relatives' marital status (e.g: co-habiting, being married or same-sex partnerships/relationships).

Creating your genogram also provides essential demographics about family members and relatives (e.g: age, age of death, and composition of families). From it, you can also identify patterns (e.g: disabilities, early deaths, favouritism) and history of relationships (e.g: having children from multiple partners, multi-relational groups, polygamy/polyandry).

Furthermore, it depicts inter-generational family maps in an attempt to create a picture of the dynamics across families and generations, thereby, providing a broad framework with which to view interactions among various family members.

Additionally, it provides a medical history of the members in areas such as physical illnesses and various forms of language or societal problems (e.g: incarceration).

Focus your attention on ages of deaths, divorces, marriages, co-habiting (ie living together) relationships and those you have migrated and are living overseas.

TASK 1:

Resume the work on your **Genogram** and continue working on it as best as you can. Attempt to work through the areas mentioned above (e.g: age of deaths). Include names, ages, children and those who are living abroad.

TASK 2

Turn to the Assessment and Evaluation Tools Kit and take some time to complete the **Psychological Self-care and Wellness Assessment** relating to your psychological health. As you work through the statements, seek to be as honest as possible and be very demanding on yourself.

Personal Reflective Session (WEEK 10)

- In relation to your emotional health, how effective was the creation of your genogram? What significant insight have you gained? (**For example**: *Have you recognised unwholesome relational patterns in your family/with your relatives? Have you recognised patterns which you are engaging in unintentionally?*)

....

....

....

....

....

....

- What dysfunctional issues in your life/ (in your family/ among your relatives) have you identified, from your genogram that need addressing?

....

....

....

....

....

....

- In what way have these dysfunctional issues been impacting on your life over the **last year**?

....

....

....

....

....

- Turn to **Page 31** in the *Set the Captives Free* Resource Guide/Manual and examine the model. Which level are you at on the pyramid?

....

....

....

....

....

....

....

....

....

....

....

- Describe two (2) actions you would need to take or processes you need to engage in so that you can move up to the next level on the pyramid?

....

....

....

....

....

....

....

....

....

....

VICTOR MARSHALL

Emotional Health Lifestyle Scorecard

Week _____

ACTIVITY	DAY OF THE WEEK AND DATE						
	Sun ----/----/----	Mon ----/----/----	Tues ----/----/----	Wed ----/----/----	Thurs ----/----/----	Fri ----/----/----	Sat ----/----/----
Spiritual Engagement * Prepare for the journey of restoration with spiritual practices (See *Set the Captives Free Workbook*, pp.15, 73							
Relationship Building Pray for a particular family member/relative/friend with whom you are having difficulty							
Exercise Engage in Exercise. State the type and amount of time daily							
Goal-setting Identify two or three things you wish to accomplish daily AND MONTHLY. This inspires hope and optimism in that you would have accomplished a goal							
Discussion Time * Identify any two (2) issues to be addressed with a particular family member/relative/friend, and prayerfully talk to that person about the issues							
Personal Reflection How much time have you spent on the reflection activity at the end of each **SESSION**?							
Special Reading On a daily basis, read ten (10) verses from the Gospel of St Mark 1-12. Also identify and **MEMORISE** the verse that attracts you. .... *Favourite Verse(s)*	*Verses Read*	*Verses Read*	*Verses Read*	*Verses Read*	*Verses Read*	*Verses Read*	*Verses Read* ....
Water How many glasses of water did you drink during the day?							

NOTE: * Place a tick (√) in the box next to these items to show that you have completed the activity on a daily basis. It is expected that these activities will take time and will be on-going.

NOTES

Feel free to use this space to write out the verse you are memorising from the chapter you have read this week, as a way of helping you internalise the text.

Session Eleven

Fulfilling Psychological Needs Enhances Emotional Health

During this session, pay attention to:

1) The connection between Adverse Childhood Experiences (ACEs) and Maslow's Hierarchy of Needs.

2) Health-enhancing interventions to counteract the negative impact of ACEs

3) The steps involved in the five stages for addressing relational issues

You will notice in your workbook that you have the outline of the PowerPoint presentation for **Session Eleven**, so that you may follow along.

DVD/PowerPoint Slides

Session Eleven

Fulfilling Psychological Needs Enhances Emotional Health

During the PowerPoint presentations, feel free to follow along with the slides that correspond with those in the session. You can fill in the blank spaces with the missing words. Use the blanks in the margin with the letters that match to the letters on the blanks in the PowerPoint slides. (For example, for blank [a], write the answer on the line next to the section of the slide marked [a].

1.

> # EMOTIONAL HEALTH RESTORATION PROGRAMME
>
> Identifying Emotional Dys-functionality and Possible Solutions

2.

> ## Session 11
>
> Fulfilling Psychological Needs Enhances Emotional Health

Categories of Adverse Childhood Experiences (ACEs)

Researchers, focusing on Adverse Childhood Experiences have identify the most common ones in their studies. These are:

- types of abuse such as emotional and ___**a**___,
- **loss** (e.g: death of a significant other, sibling)
- ___**b**__ (e.g: lack of emotional or physical care)
- household dysfunctionality (e.g: incarcerated of family member, or _____**c**_____).

Willis, G. M. & Levenson, J. S. (2016). The relationship between childhood adversity and adult psychosocial outcomes in females who have sexually offended: implications for treatment. *Journal of Sexual Aggression*, 22(3), pp.355-367 (356).

3.

a. _____

b. _____

c. _____

Prevalence of ACEs I

Research has shown a strong positive ____**d**____between mental health problems (e.g: self-harm) and childhood abuse and neglect. 912 children in the American welfare system, aged 1.5 to 5.11 years, were studied. The results revealed that

- half of the children (50.5%) experienced four or more ACEs,
- around three-quarters experienced emotional (78.0%) or physical (70.8%) abuse.

Kerker, B. D., Zhang, J., Nadeem, E., Stein, R. E. K. et al (2015). Adverse Childhood Experiences and Mental Health, Chronic Medical Conditions, and Development in Young Children. *Academic Pediatrics*,15 (5), pp. 510-517.

4.

d. _____

Impact of ACEs: Mental Health issues

The study of Kerker et al. also revealed that 98.1 % of the children had experienced at least one ACE. Further, the researchers found that a higher number of ACES before age 5 was associated with a greater likelihood of mental health and chronic medical problems. Importantly, the relationship between ACEs and ____**e**____ development was only significant among 3–5 year-olds. These data highlight the prevalence of adverse experiences among very young children in a most ____**f**____ population.

Kerker, Zhang et al., 'Adverse Childhood Experiences and Mental Health, Chronic Medical Conditions, and Development in Young Children'.

5.

e. _____

f. _____

The Twelve 'Risk' Categories

1. Emotional Instability	7. Unresolved Issues
2. Emotional Hurt	8. Inability to Cope
3. Lifestyle	9. Medical Condition
4. Nutrition	10. Childhood Adversity
5. Unforgiveness	11. **Psychological Needs**
6. Abuse	12. Mental Functioning

6.

ACEs and Maslow's Hierarchy of Needs I

Individuals have basic needs which are categorised as:

- physiological (e.g: clothing, food, sleep), and
- safety (e.g: family stability, health and personal security).
- Additionally, there are other needs, namely
- psychological (e.g: acceptance by others, family connection,) and
- esteem needs (e.g: achievements, and self-worth).

These are ____g____ needs because of ____h____ hence the motivation to fulfil them.

Noltemeyer, A. Bush, K., Patton, J. and Bergen, D. (2012). The relationship among deficiency needs and growth needs: An empirical investigation of Maslow's theory. *Children and Youth Services Review,* 34 (9), pp.1862-1867 (1862).

7.

g. _____

h. _____

ACEs and Maslow's Hierarchy of Needs II

Children who experience various types of abuse would have been denied personal security or protection, and by extension, have unmet ____i____ needs. Furthermore, those who experienced neglect would have been hindered from developing a sense of belonging or building family connections. This highlights the prevalence of unmet physiological needs (e.g: lack of food) or psychological needs in terms of love. Consequently, children who undergo adverse experiences have various types of deficiency needs.

Noltemeyer et al., The relationship among deficiency needs and growth needs', p. 1862.

8.

i. _____

ACEs and Safety Needs

Physical abuse signals disrespect from others, where children are not being valued, thus, an example of unmet esteem needs. This type of abuse also demonstrates that children's safety needs have been ignored, seeing that they lack protection from sexual predators. Furthermore, an ___j___ home (e.g: parental violence) pinpoints family insecurity, while sick children left unattended, can experience poor health and well-being, another example of unmet safety needs which can impact on cognitive competence.

Noltemeyer et al., The relationship among deficiency needs and growth needs', p. 1863.

9.

j. _____

ACEs and Belonging Needs I

Various ACEs revolve around poor relationship issues, which bring about traumas in children's lives. A lack of clothing indicates physical neglect, while abandonment/parental absence or social isolation are evidence of ___k___ neglect. The study of Chakhssi et al. indicates that child sexual offenders have experienced disconnection, rejection and social isolation from adults more than sexual offenders against adults or non-sexual offenders in their early years. This suggests they have a deficiency in love and belonging needs.

Chakhssi, F., de Ruiter, C., & Bernstein, D. P. (2013). Early Maladaptive Cognitive Schemas in Child Sexual Offenders Compared with Sexual Offenders against Adults and Nonsexual Violent Offenders: An Exploratory Study. The Journal of Sexual Medicine, 10(9), 2201–2210 (2206).

10.

k. _____

ACEs and Belonging Needs II

ACEs such as sexual abuse (e.g: incest, exposure to or participation in pornography) is evidence of misplaced intimacy, and inappropriate affection towards children. Being ostracized by parents is indicative of their ___l___, whereas bullying and school violence suggests poor interpersonal relationship were left unaddressed. Such experiences highlight the perspective that home is emotionally ___m___, hence children lack a sense of belonging.

Oral, R., Ramirez, M., Coohey, C., Nakada, S., Walz, A., Kuntz, A., Benoit, J. & Peek-Asa Adverse childhood experiences and trauma informed care: the future of health care. *Pediatric Research,* 79 **(1),** 227–233 (227)

11.

l. _____

m. _____

Impact of ACEs on Psychological Needs

Exposure to ACEs prevent children from accessing basic needs (e.g: adequate sleep and personal protection), and eventually hinder the ___**n**___ of psychological needs (e.g: appreciation, confidence, friendship and self-esteem). In particular, an undeveloped sense of belonging explains the relationship between previous experiences of adversity and more direct manifestations of psychological distress such as depression.

Corrales, T., Waterford, M., Goodwin-Smith, I., Wood, L., Yourell, T., & Ho, C. (2016). Childhood adversity, sense of belonging and psychosocial outcomes in emerging adulthood: A test of mediated pathways. *Children and Youth Services Review*, 63, 110–119 (116).

12.

n. _____

Fulfilling Psychological Needs: Volunteering

Individuals who volunteer with an organisation are developing a sense of pride and have feelings of being respected. Additionally, volunteering is psychologically beneficial, seeing that it leads to

- community empowerment, great "connectedness,"
- an improved sense of community,
- group membership which develops our ____**o**___ and
- developing a meaningful sense of belonging to social groups.

Gray, D. & Stevenson, C. (2020). How can 'we' help? Exploring the role of shared social identity in the experiences and benefits of volunteering. *Journal of Community and Applied Social Psychology*, 30(4), pp. 341-353 (342, 343,344).

13.

o. _____

Volunteering Improves Sense of Belonging: Evidence

A study was conducted with 33 mainly Caucasian (98%) British volunteers. Their average age was 56.44%, with 67.5% being females. There was an equal number of retirees and students (28.12%), while more than one-fifth was full-time employees (21.9%). Findings indicate that volunteering aided a sense of ___**p**__. It provided:

- feelings of acceptance and a sense of belonging that shapes their needs and desires to volunteer.
- a source of identity-based support and a means of ___**q**____.

Gray & Stevenson, 'How can 'we' help? Exploring the role of shared social identity in the experiences and benefits of volunteering', p. 350.

14.

p. _____

q. _____

Goal Setting Impacts Esteem Needs

104 patients (70 % females) with neuro-muscular disorders (e.g: muscular dystrophy) and receiving physiotherapy, completed a survey. 60% was in the 36-65 age group, and 60 % was attending physiotherapy for more than 5 years. Data showed that 28% of goals set, focused on ___r___ and living with the condition by

  i.   improving their emotional state, and

  ii. building ____s___ to perform home exercise activities.

Goal-setting enables physiotherapists to ___t__ patients and develop patients' self-management skills.

Hartley, S. E & Stockley, R. C. (2016). Collaborative goal setting with adults attending physiotherapy at a specialist neuromuscular centre: is it always appropriate? A cross-sectional survey. *Physiotherapy*, 102 (4), 320-326.

15.

r. _____

s. _____

t. _____

Effect of Music Therapy

A review was done using 36 studies relating to the impact of music therapy on traumatic experiences such as ACEs. The findings revealed that _____u_____ (e.g: listening to music, singing, relaxing with music) provided various benefits such as:

- developing a sense of self-worth, sleep and/or relaxation
- symptom reduction, resilience and empowerment,
- community building, facilitating grieving, relaxation, reflection, socialization, and _____v_____.

McFerran, K. S., Lai, H. I. C.,Chang, WH., Acquaro, D. et al (2020). Music, Rhythm and Trauma: A Critical Interpretive Synthesis of Research Literature. *Frontiers in Psychology*, 11 (324).

16.

u. _____

v. _____

Impact of Music: Evidence

A study was done with 50 hemodialysis patients (54% females), ages 30-65 and 86 % being married. Mental disorders, if not diagnosed and managed well, can create low quality of life in the patients, poor adherence to hemodialysis treatment, and increased death rate among patients. Results showed a decrease in anxiety and depression scores after music therapy with the intervention group, while the control group, before and after the intervention, had no significant difference.

Imani, M., Jalali, A., Salari, N., Abbasi, P. (2021). Effect of instrumental music on anxiety and depression among hemodialysis patients: A randomized controlled trial. *Journal of Education Health Promotions,* 10(305).

17.

Biblical Insight

An important purpose for which Christ ____**w**____ death on the Cross was to ____**x**____ each human being back to the Divine Creator. We are reminded that "all things are from God, Who through *Jesus* Christ reconciled us to Himself [received us into favor, brought us into harmony with Himself] and gave to us the ministry of reconciliation [that by word and deed we might aim to bring others into harmony with Him]"

2 Cor 5:18, AMP).

18.

w. _____

x. _____

Addressing Unresolved Underlying Issues

STAGE 1
Facing Unresolved Past Issues

19.

Stage I: Acknowledge the Problem

This stage requires us to agree or recognise that an adverse relational issue has occurred. In contrast, refusing to see the unresolved issue leads to ____**y**____. It is a defence mechanism, used by individuals, in trying to cope with an unpleasant or unexpected situation, which is difficult to accept as being true. It also results in the individual refusing assistance (e.g: medical aid, therapy) which tends to be detrimental to our health and well-being.

Marshall, V. D. (2013). *Set the captives free: Experiencing healing through holistic restoration* (Bloomington, IN: AuthorHouse), p.59; Kallergis, G. (2008). Using the denial mechanism to inform the cancer patient. *JBOUN*, 13 (4), pp.559-563 (559).

20.

y. _____

Scientific Evidence

A study was done with 361 Dutch workers (54.3% males), whose average age was 43.1 years and where 79.3 % have at least a high school diploma. Results indicated that ___z___ coping strategies (e.g: denial) are associated with more health complaints and more depression. Employees who experience bullying and who frequently use these strategies to deal with problems at work do not seem to benefit from these approaches to coping, seeing that bullying co-exists with more health complaints, more depressive symptoms, poorer well-being, and greater absenteeism.

Dehue, F., Bolman, C., Völlink, T., & Pouwelse, M. (2012). Coping with bullying at work and health related problems. *International Journal of Stress Management, 19*(3), 175–197 (191).

21.

z. _____

Addressing Unresolved Underlying Issues

STAGE 1
Facing Unresolved Past Issues

STAGE 2
Beware of Consequences

22.

Stage 2: Addressing Unresolved Underlying Issues

Unresolved adverse experiences bring consequences due to broken relationships. These can be categorised as
- emotional (e.g: anger, fear),
- physiological such as liver disease,
- _____a2_____ (e,g: suicidal tendencies) and
- social (e.g: criminality, promiscuity, unwanted pregnancies).

Being aware pinpoints areas in one's life to be addressed.

Turner S, Harvey C, Hayes L, Castle D, Galletly C, Sweeney S, Shah S, Keogh L, Spittal MJ (2020). Childhood adversity and clinical and psychosocial outcomes in psychosis. Epidemiology and Psychiatric Sciences 29, e78, 1–10 (2).; Marshall, *Set the captives free: Experiencing healing through holistic restoration*, pp. 60-61.

23.

a2._____

Addressing Unresolved Underlying Issues

24.

```
┌─────────────────────┐
│      STAGE 1        │
│ Facing Unresolved Past │
│       Issues        │
└─────────────────────┘
            │
            ▼
    ┌─────────────────┐
    │    STAGE 2      │
    │ Beware of Consequences │
    └─────────────────┘
            │
            ▼
    ┌─────────────────┐
    │    STAGE 3      │
    │ Exchange Consequences │
    │    for Virtues   │
    └─────────────────┘
```

Stage 3: Develop Virtues

Adverse emotional experiences render us to be _____**b2**_____, distrusting and resentful. However, to rebuild broken relational bridges require qualities such as honesty, humility, and open-ness. It is an opportunity to spend time in _____**c2**_____ where we seek to make the _____**d2**_____ of relinquishing negative emotions for positive virtues and qualities. Acquiring these qualities require a willingness to be intentional about progressing and becoming transformed.

Marshall, *Set the captives free: Experiencing healing through holistic restoration*, pp. 62-63.

25.

b2._____

c2._____

d2._____

Addressing Unresolved Underlying Issues

26.

```
┌─────────────────────┐
│      STAGE 1        │
│ Facing Unresolved Past │
│       Issues        │
└─────────────────────┘
            │
            ▼
    ┌─────────────────┐
    │    STAGE 2      │
    │ Beware of Consequences │
    └─────────────────┘
            │
            ▼
┌─────────────┐   ┌─────────────────┐
│   STAGE 4   │◄──│    STAGE 3      │
│ Experience  │   │ Exchange Consequences │
│ Relational  │   │    for Virtues   │
│  Healing    │   └─────────────────┘
└─────────────┘
```

VICTOR MARSHALL

Stage 4: Experience Relational Healing

Stage 4 of this journey requires us to develop a harmonious relationship by extending forgiveness, thereby preparing for emotional and spiritual healing. Extending forgiveness leads to reconciliation, which entails ___**e2**___ the exhibition of negative emotions such as anger for a display of wholesome positive emotions (e.g: peace) and an engagement of healthy interactions.

Marshall, *Set the captives free: Experiencing healing through holistic restoration*, p.62.

27.

e2. _____

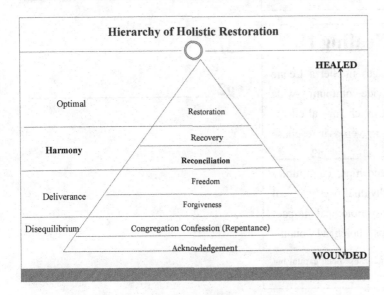

Hierarchy of Holistic Restoration

HEALED

Optimal	Restoration
	Recovery
Harmony	**Reconciliation**
	Freedom
Deliverance	Forgiveness
Disequilibrium	Congregation Confession (Repentance)
	Acknowledgement

WOUNDED

28.

Divine-Human Disconnect

Broken relationships between individuals are indicative of a broken relationship with the Divine Healer. This view is grounded biblically in that whoever claims to be in connection with the Healing Redeemer, but displays detestable attitudes and behaviours towards his fellowman, he/she is experiencing internal ____**f2**____. There is a spiritual disconnect when individuals believe they have a healthy relationship with the Invisible Divine One, but is displeased with and engage in unwholesome interactions with fellow human beings.

1 John 4:20 NIV.

29.

f2. _____

Reconciliation and Healing I

Reconciliation can impact positively seeing that it may improve psychological health if sharing accounts has a cleansing effect. There are negative psychological consequences (e.g: being traumatic) because painful memories are awakened. Reconciliation processes may also:

- affect societal healing through their effects on social capital.
- be aimed at forgiving former perpetrators,
- rebuild and increase trust toward former combatants.

Cilliers, J., Dube, O. and Siddiqi, B. (2016). Reconciling after civil conflict increases social capital but decreases individual well-being. *Science*, 352 (6287), pp. 787-794 (787-789).

30.

Reconciliation and Healing II

A study was conducted with 200 villages in Sierra Leone which were impacted by civil war to provide community-wide reconciliation. The results indicated that psychological effects did not prevent individuals who extended forgiveness in response to reconciliation from gaining psychological _____g2_____. The gains in societal healing (e.g friendships, community contribution) were costly in terms of individual psychological healing. Additionally, the negative psychological impact occurred because truth-telling opened up psychological wounds.

Cilliers et al, 'Reconciling after civil conflict increases social capital but decreases individual well-being., pp.791, 794..

31.

g2. _____

Reconciliation and Healing III

22 employees of an American Children's Welfare agency shared their experience of a reconciliation process which was set up to address workplace challenges. The findings indicate that

- individuals are helped to move beyond the crisis moments to recognize positive outcomes in the work,
- intrapersonal reconciliation facilitates a self-referential process where employees need to make sense of the difficult experiences and then identify how to continue making meaningful service contributions.

Carol Flinchbaugh, Catherine Schwoerer & Douglas R. May (2016): Helping yourself to help others: how cognitive change strategies improve employee reconciliation with service clients and positive work outcomes, *Journal of Change Management,* 17 (3), pp.249-267.

32.

Addressing Unresolved Underlying Issues

33.

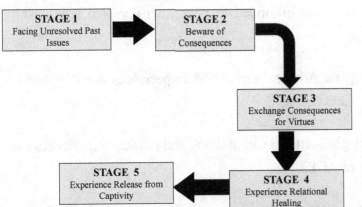

STAGE 1
Facing Unresolved Past Issues

STAGE 2
Beware of Consequences

STAGE 3
Exchange Consequences for Virtues

STAGE 4
Experience Relational Healing

STAGE 5
Experience Release from Captivity

Stage 5: Experience Release from Captivity

34.

h2._____

In the context of forgiveness, healing and reconciliation occur. Reconciliation indicates that inter-relational ___h2___ exists, in that, there is release from emotional, psychological and spiritual captivity created by the consequences of ACEs. The journey of rebuilding broken relational bridges enables us to adjust our perspectives about others, and reinstate values such as acceptance and tolerance. This allows us to progress and move forward in pursuit of other health-promoting and health-enhancing goals.

Marshall, *Set the captives free: Experiencing healing through holistic restoration*, p.63.

Social Relationships Promote Harmony

35.

We sustain a loss when we neglect the privilege of associating together to strengthen and encourage one another in the service of God. Our hearts cease to be enlightened and aroused by their sanctifying influence, and we decline in spirituality. In our association as Christians, we lose much by lack of sympathy with one another. He who shuts himself up to himself is not filling the position that God designed he should. The proper cultivation of the social elements in our nature brings us into sympathy with others and is a means of development and strength to us in the service of God.

White, E. G. (2000). *Mind, Character & Personality Vol. 2* (Hagerstown, MD: Review & Herald Publishing Association), p.622.

Summary

➢ Adverse Childhood Experiences are grounded in poor inter-personal relationship issues.

➢ Individuals who have undergone Adverse Childhood Experiences are deficient in Maslow's basic and psychological needs.

➢ Various interventions such as goal-setting, volunteering and musical experiences can counteract the consequences of ACEs.

➢ Dysfunctional relational patterns can also be counteracted by engaging in the 5-stage process for Addressing relational issues.

Insightful Perspectives

a) Remember to take some time to go through the Section entitled 'A Journey Towards Reconciliation on **pages 62-63** in *Set the Captives Free (Resource Guide).*

b) Turn to Chapter 11 and engage in the week's reading –'Private-Keep Out!' in *Raising the Wounded: Grasping for Hope in the Midst of Despair.*

Emotional Healthy Lifestyle Matters

Let's turn to the *emotional healthy lifestyle matters* section. These are activities and tasks we can engage in as a means of aiding our emotional, intellectual physical, psychological, relational, social and spiritual development. Some of these can be done on your own at home.

1. Music Intervention

Garrido, Baker et al. (2015) noted that musical experiences such as singing and listening to music (e.g: hymns, classical and instrumentals) allow individuals to express their emotions and feelings in a healthy and healing way about various issues such as natural disasters. Music has also been used to aid individuals in becoming confident, upbeat, and optimistic.

SOURCE: Garrido, S., Baker, F. A., Davidson, J. W., Moore, G. and Wasserman, S. (2015). Music and trauma: the relationship between music, personality, and coping style. *Frontiers in Psychology*, 6(977).

TASK 1

Set your music equipment play, while you listen to at least one Gospel instrumental song/hymn three days per week for five (5) minutes each day.

TASK 2

Listen to and sing at least one Gospel hymn/song or health-promoting song four (4) days a week for five (5) minutes per day

(a) Reflect on how you felt **DURING** the singing of the hymns/songs.

....

....

....

....

....

....

....

2. Building Relationships

Healthy and positive interpersonal relationships require a display of wholesome attitudes and behaviours and healthy interactions with others. In **Sessions 9 & 10,** we embarked on seeking to achieve harmony by rebuilding broken relationship bridges. In this **Session,** it is important to continue applying the various biblical principles which we have encountered while addressing these emotional issues. The material relating to the Journey Towards Reconciliation is useful for this objective.

TASK 1:

a) In your *Set the Captives free: 12 Studies for Individuals or Groups* Workbook, on **pages 82 – 87,** you will find activities to assist you in continuing on the Journey Towards Reconciliation, in order to experience peace and harmony. Work through the activities on these pages as you continue on your journey.

3. Goal-setting

Individuals who seek to set goals receive benefits such as an improvement in their emotional state, building confidence in performing various activities. Additionally, goal-setting is a self-management strategy used by individuals who have medical conditions.

TASK 1:

Review the various tasks relating to setting of goals on **Pages 59, 123, 147 and 233** in this *Companion Workbook.* Take the time to work through the different goals and seek to create the opportunity to achieve your realistic and timely goals.

4. Assessment

As you continue to work on your genogram, you would have noticed that it allowed you to identify and evaluate family dynamics such as marital status and various familial patterns (e.g: inter-generational dynamics).

Creating your genogram also enables you to understand the relational issues, emotional relationships and medical history. This type of history provides a medical context in which you and your immediate family exist. Furthermore, the genogram allows you to delve deeper into your family background and unearth unknown or unusual information. From it, you can also identify patterns (e.g: family secrets, life span and family health), along with interactional patterns which existed in at least three generations.

Focus your attention on medical issues (e.g: disabilities, substance misuse, mental health issues, physical health issues (e.g: diabetics).

TASK 1:

Resume the work on your **Genogram** and continue working on it as best as you can. Attempt to work through the areas mentioned above (e.g: physical health). Include specific issues such as visual impairment, and speech difficulties.

5. Review from Previous Sessions

In the last three (3) weeks, you have taken into account various *emotional healthy lifestyle matters*, all relating to nutrition, forgiveness and emotional freedom. These areas are listed below. Please circle the answer for each activity to indicate whether or not you have been taking part in these activities. The superscript number indicates the *Session* where each lifestyle matter is found.

Select moody foods[10]	Doing	Not Doing
Engage in spiritual disciplines (meditation/reflection)[10]	Doing	Not Doing
Building relationships[8,9,10]	Doing	Not Doing
Building resilience[8]	Doing	Not Doing
Implement goals for psychological self-care[10]	Doing	Not Doing
Flushing the mind through wholesome activities[10]	Doing	Not Doing
Adequate water intake[8,9]	Doing	Not Doing
Practise goal-setting[6,7]	Doing	Not Doing
Physical Exercise[8,9]	Doing	Not Doing
Sleep and Diet Detox[10]	Doing	Not Doing
Creating a genogram[9,10]	Doing	Not Doing
Massage Therapy[10]	Doing	Not Doing
Replacing Negative Views/Thoughts[8]	Doing	Not Doing

Plans & Goal Setting

On the lines below, write out **a plan for each Lifestyle activity** you need to adopt /start to practise from the list above. State the possible time of the day or of the week (e.g morning, afternoon; weekends) that you will seek to incorporate your new habits.

Alternatively, review the plans that you may have set out for yourself in Session 4 on **Pages 80-81**, and in Session 8 on **Pages 167-168**. Share how you plan to begin implementing YOUR previous plans for each of the activities you marked **NOT DOING.**

Also, review the suggestions given in the **Emotional Healthy Lifestyle Section** of each previous week, as stated in this *Companion Folder*

Setting out My Plans & Goals

....

....

....

....

....

....

....

....

....

....

....

....

....

....

....

....

....

....

....

....

....

....

....

....

VICTOR MARSHALL

....

....

....

....

....

....

....

....

....

....

....

....

....

....

....

....

....

....

....

....

....

....

....

....

Personal Reflective Session (WEEK 11)

- Take a few moments to review your genogram? Identify three (3) dysfunctional patterns from your genogram which you would like to address.

....

....

....

....

....

....

....

....

....

....

- Discus and share three (3) practical ways you can address/break the dysfunctional patterns which you have identified above.

....

....

....

....

....

....

....

....

....

....

- What adverse experiences have you had as a result of the dysfunctional patterns you have identified in your family, if applicable.

....
....
....
....
....
....
....
....
....
....
....
....

- Share two ways in which these dysfunctional issues have been impacting on your life over the **last year**?

....
....
....
....
....
....
....
....
....
....
....

Emotional Health Lifestyle Scorecard

Week _____

ACTIVITY	DAY OF THE WEEK AND DATE						
	Sun ----/----/-----	Mon ----/----/----	Tues ----/----/----	Wed ----/----/----	Thurs ----/----/----	Fri ----/----/----	Sat ----/----/----
Spiritual Engagement * Prepare for the journey of restoration with spiritual practices (See *Set the Captives Free Workbook*, pp.15, 73							
Relationship Building Pray for a particular family member/relative/friend with whom you are having difficulty							
Exercise Engage in Exercise. State the type and amount of time daily							
Goal-setting Identify two or three things you wish to accomplish daily AND MONTHLY. This inspires hope and optimism in that you would have accomplished a goal							
Discussion Time * Identify any two (2) issues to be addressed with a particular family member/relative/friend, and prayerfully talk to that person about the issues							
Personal Reflection How much time have you spent on the reflection activity at the end of each **SESSION**?							
Special Reading On a daily basis, read ten (10) verses from the Gospel of St Mark 1-12. Also identify and **MEMORISE** the verse that attracts you. *Favourite Verse(s)*	*Verses Read*	*Verses Read*	*Verses Read*	*Verses Read*	*Verses Read*	*Verses Read*	*Verses Read* ....
Water How many glasses of water did you drink during the day?							

NOTE: * Place a tick (√) in the box next to these items to show that you have completed the activity on a daily basis. It is expected that these activities will take time and will be on-going.

VICTOR MARSHALL

NOTES

Feel free to use this space to write out the verse you are memorising from the chapter you have read this week, as a way of helping you internalise the text.

Session Twelve

How to Improve Brain Function

During this session, pay attention to:

1) The regions of the human brain which are affected by ACEs.

2) Events which lead to damaged regions of the prefrontal cortex and limbic system.

3) Interventions which can repair damaged regions of the brain.

You will notice in your workbook that you have the outline of the PowerPoint presentation for **Session Twelve**, so that you may follow along.

DVD/PowerPoint Slides

Session Twelve

How to Improve Brain Function

During the PowerPoint presentations, feel free to follow along with the slides that correspond with those in the session. You can fill in the blank spaces with the missing words. Use the blanks in the margin with the letters that match to the letters on the blanks in the PowerPoint slides. (For example, for blank [a], write the answer on the line next to the section of the slide marked [a].

1.

> ## EMOTIONAL HEALTH RESTORATION PROGRAMME
>
> Identifying Emotional Dys-functionality and Possible Solutions

2.

> ## Session 12
>
> How to Improve Brain Function

Categories of Adverse Childhood Experiences

Researchers, in their studies, focus on the most common Adverse Childhood Experiences namely: abuses (e.g: emotional, physical, sexual):

- family dysfunctionality (e.g: criminality, divorce, domestic violence, substance abuse)
- loss through death or migration
- neglect (e.g: emotional)
- psychological difficulties (e.g: mental illness)
- social problems (e.g: poverty, low socio-economic status).

Oral, R., Ramirez, M., Coohey, C., Nakada, S., Walz, A., Kuntz, A., Benoit, J. & Peek-Asa, C. (2015). Adverse childhood experiences and trauma informed care: the future of health care. *Pediatric Research*, 79 (1), 227–233 (227).

3.

Impact of ACEs on Mental Health

Research has shown that Adverse Childhood Experiences have impacted individuals' mental health in their ___a___. A study involving 7 465 American outpatients (53.3% females and 75.2% Caucasians), examined the relationship between ACEs and adult mental health outcomes. The results indicated that as ACE score ___b___ the odds of experiencing substance misuse (e.g: drug and alcohol), suicide attempts, and depressed affect in adulthood also increased.

Merricka, M. T., Portsa, K. A., Forda, D. C., Afifib, T. O., Gershoffc , E. T. and Grogan-Kaylord, A. (2017). *Child Abuse & Neglect*, 69, pp.10-19.

4.

a. _____

b. _____

The Twelve 'Risk' Categories

1. Emotional Instability	7. Unresolved Issues
2. Emotional Hurt	8. Inability to Cope
3. Lifestyle	9. Medical Condition
4. Nutrition	10. Childhood Adversity
5. Unforgiveness	11. Psychological Needs
6. Abuse	12. **Mental Functioning**

5.

ACEs Affect the __c__

Adverse Childhood Experiences lead to various types of physiological (e.g: obesity), psychological (e.g: addictions) and social (e.g: promiscuous) outcomes which ultimately contribute to a _____d_____ or defective pre-frontal cortex (PFC). Children's brain injuries (e.g: skull bruises or fractures), or bio-chemical events, because of traumas or lack of oxygen at birth, tend to result in an impaired PFC. This impaired area of the brain, if left unaddressed, can negatively affects our mental health and well-being throughout adulthood.

6.

c. _____

d. _____

Brain Anatomy I

The human brain consists of three main parts:

- _____e_____
- cerebellum and the
- __f___

The cerebrum has the outer grey matter (cerebral cortex), an inner mass of white matter and subcortical structures.

7.

e. _____

f. _____

Parts of the Human Brain

8.

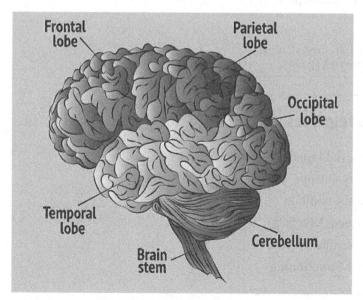

Frontal lobe

Parietal lobe

Occipital lobe

Temporal lobe

Cerebellum

Brain stem

Brain Anatomy II

The cerebrum (forebrain) is the largest part of the brain and is divided into:
- left and right _____g_____.

Each hemisphere has:
- ___h____ cortex (cortex of the brain) and
- subcortical ___i___ (e.g: limbic structures, pituitary gland).

9.

g. _____

h. _____

i. _____

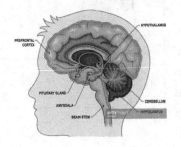

Location of the Prefrontal Cortex

10.

Location of the Pre-frontal Cortex

The prefrontal cortex is located to the ___j___ of the brain in the frontal lobe and behind the forehead. The PFC is connected to the brain's motor and pre-motor areas.

I. The PFC is the last part of the brain to form and takes a longer period to develop.

II. The development of the PFC ends around age 25.

III. The brain develops from back to front, resulting in the front part taking longer.

11.

j. _____

Functions of Pre-frontal Cortex

Scientific studies reveal that the prefrontal cortex:

- carries out ___k___ functions (e.g: store and retrieve memory; maintain attention and focus; assesses and rationalizes thoughts and assists with decision-making)
- assists with ___l___ regulation (e.g: self-control), and complex behavioural and cognitive functions
- moderates social behaviour
- engages in personality expression and
- aids with ___m___ and morality.

Lee, D., & Seo, H. (2007). Mechanisms of Reinforcement Learning and Decision Making in the Primate Dorsolateral Prefrontal Cortex. Annals of the New York Academy of Sciences, 1104(1), 108–122 (116).

12.

k. _____

l. _____

m. _____

Contributing Factors to Damaged PFC

During psychological stress, the amygdala ___n___ stress pathways in the hypothalamus and brainstem, evoking hormone release (e.g: dopamine). This impairs PFC regulation (e.g: attention regulation), but strengthens amygdala function. Chronic ___o___ during brain development/childhood affects the PFC structure and function into adulthood. Adverse issues in childhood tend to contribute to formal mental illnesses. Also, genetic and environmental factors (e.g: toxins from cocaine) can dysregulate stress signalling pathways in the PFC, weaken its abilities and bring on symptoms of ___p___ illness.

Arnsten, A. F. T. (2009). Stress signalling pathways that impair prefrontal cortex structure and function. Nature reviews. Neuroscience, 10(6), pp.410–422.

13.

n. _____

o. _____

p. _____

Effects of an Impaired Prefrontal Cortex

An impaired prefrontal cortex results in:

- Inattention, lack of concentration, disorganisation in daily tasks
- ___q___ behaviour because of emotional dys-regulation.
- Psychiatric disorders and neurological conditions.

Friedman, et al. (2021). The role of prefrontal cortex in cognitive control and executive function. *Neuropsychopharmacology*, 47, pp.72–89 (72).

14.

q. _____

Treatment for Damaged PFC: Music Therapy

Twenty-three moderate-to-severe traumatic ____r____ injury (TBI) patients, being in the 16-60 age-group, and who were injured for up to 2 years, were involved in a study. They underwent 20 individual music ____s____ sessions. The findings indicate that the music therapy strengthened network connectivity between the frontoparietal and dorsal attention, while there was cognitive ____t____ in executive function.

Martínez-Molina, N et al. (2021)., "Resting-State Network Plasticity Induced by Music Therapy after Traumatic Brain Injury", *Neural Plasticity.*

Brain Care

In order to achieve optimal functioning in the prefrontal cortex individuals should:

- Consume protein-rich foods
- Include foods which provide micro-nutrients (e.g: iron, zinc)
- Engage in physical activity,
- Ensure the brain gets adequate ____u____.
- Avoid being physically injured.

Cusick, et al.. (2016). The Role of Nutrition in Brain Development: The Golden Opportunity of the "First 1000 Days". *Journal of Pediatrics*, 175, pp.16-21.

Spirituality and Prefrontal Cortex

A review of 96 articles was done to examine cortical change through meditation and religiosity and /or spirituality. Results indicate that religious practices (e.g: prayer, spiritual meditation) improved ____v____ and well-being, both of which are tied to neurological changes in the prefrontal region and its connection to subcortical structures (e.g: limbic structures-amygdala). Furthermore, prefrontal lobe change led to positive ____w____ and emotional changes.

Barnby, J. M., Bailey, N. W., Chambers, R. and Fitzgerald, P. B. (2015). How similar are the changes in neural activity resulting from mindfulness practice in contrast to spiritual practice? *Consciousness and Cognition*, 36, pp.219-232 (228).

15.

r. _____

s. _____

t. _____

16.

u. _____

17.

v. _____

w. _____

Function of the Limbic Lobe

The Limbic lobe:

- _____x_____ responses to emotions, such as the adrenaline-based fight-or-flight response.
- triggers a _____y___ to perceived danger, regulates both conscious and unconscious functions (e.g: appetite)
- attaches significance to sensory experiences by subjectively feeling emotions.
- assist with memory and learning. The hippocampus also plays key roles in visual-spatial memory,
- assists with social skills, empathy, and social processing.

18.

x. _____

y. _____

Anatomy of the Limbic System

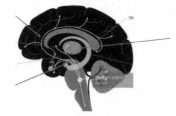

19.

z. _____

a2._____

b2._____

Functions of Sub-sections of the Limbic System

The hippocampus stores memories of various episodes which are then filed away in long-term ___m2___ It is also involved in spatial navigation, learning and emotions. The amygdala plays a role in emotional responses (e.g: anger, anxiety, fear, happiness). It interacts with the hippocampus to form _____n2_____ and attach emotional content. The hypothalamus controls automatic functions (e.g: body temperature, blood pressure, heart rate, hunger), hormones, immune system, moods and regulates sexual motivation. It also controls the body's response to stress.

20.

m2._____

n2._____

Link Between PFC and Limbic System

The prefrontal cortex connects with the limbic system (e.g amygdala, hypothalamus) so that ___o2___functions (e.g: displaying primary emotions) are integrated with higher order brain functions (e.g: calculating, motivating, thinking). The medial section builds connections with emotional processing areas of the limbic system (e.g: amygdala) and with the area for ___p2___ (e.g: hippocampus). Meanwhile, the orbito-frontal section connects with the areas involved in emotional regulation (e.g: hypothalamus).

21.

o2._____

p2._____

Damaged to the Limbic System-Hippocampus

The parts of the limbic system (e.g: hippocampus) can be damaged by
- Substance abuse (e.g: alcohol, cigarettes, drugs)
- Stress or
- _____q2_____

Prolonged and/or traumatic stressors have also been shown to cause changes in the hippocampus. In particular, studies have reported that PTSD patients had smaller hippocampal size, which links with deficits in verbal memory.

Kim, E. J., Pellman, B. and Kim, J. J. (2015). Stress effects on the hippocampus: a critical review. *Learning and Memory*,22, pp. 411-415 (413).

22.

q2._____

Damaged to the Limbic System-Hypothalamus

The parts of the limbic system (e.g: hypothalamus) can be damaged by traumatic brain injury due to
- motor vehicle accidents, falls,
- child abuse,
- violence and sports injuries.

Additionally, toxic stress as a result of _____r2_____ and adverse childhood experiences can impact negatively on the hypothalamus.

Richmond, E., Rogol, A. D. (2014). Traumatic brain injury: endocrine consequences in children and adults. *Endocrine* 45, 3–8(6); Morgan, B. (2013). Biological embedding of early childhood adversity: Toxic stress and the vicious cycle of poverty in South Africa. *Research & Policy Brief series.*

23.

r2._____

Consequences of Damaged Limbic System

Damaged areas of the limbic system can result in:

- poor decision-making
- _____s2_____
- heightened alert to threats
- _____t2_____
- loss of control of emotions
- being ____u2____ and fatigue
- puberty disturbance

Treatment for Damaged Limbic System

Various lifestyle activities such as physical exercise, and sleep _____v2____ toxins accumulated in the brain. Additionally, an iron-rich (e.g: almond nuts, spinach), high-fibre, low fat diet helps to eliminate toxins from the body. An anti-inflammatory diet is beneficial to this section of the brain. It consists of:

- Low-carbohydrate and
- low-glycemic foods,
- along with fruits and vegetables which can assist with cognitive functions.

Treatment: Music Therapy

Music therapy has a positive ____w2____ on the mood of patients suffering from different chronic illnesses (e.g: stroke). Various musical experiences (e.g: listening to instrumental music) produce stimuli which are transmitted by specific nuclei from the thalamus through the cerebral cortex, and on to the limbic system. When music is played, the parts of the limbic system are ____x2_____ to produce feelings and expressions. In a study with 59 stroke patients with moderate and severe depression, instrumental music therapy reduced the depression rates more than the other two methods.

Sumakul, V. D. O., Notobroto, H. B., Widani, N. L. and Aima, M. H. (2020). Instrumental music therapy reduced depression levels in stroke patients. *Journal of Public Health Research*, 9(1847), pp.215-218 (217).

24.

s2._____

t2._____

u2._____

25.

v2._____

26.

w2. _____

x2._____

Ancient Guidance

It is critical to have a peaceful mind which aids with personal happiness. Healthy thoughts are essential for a functional brain, which can be achieved through the power of the Healing Redeemer who is willing to "keep in perfect peace, all who trust in you, all whose thoughts are fixed on you!" This can also occur through spiritual practices such as studying and reflecting on the Sacred Word which we can use to replace negative perspectives.

Isaiah 26:3

27.

Divine Aid for Phobias

Phobia, (fears) have a weakening power whereby, they can prevent us from exploring exciting places, engaging in uplifting activities and experiencing _____**y2**_____ in various aspects of our life. Our Divine Healer instructs us to trust Him and develop confidence in Him, by not endorsing a fearful mindset. He has promised to empower us with His Holy Spirit and to help us overcome our difficulties.

Isaiah 41:10

28.

y2._____

Insightful Counsel

Continuous negative experiences tend to create distorted and negative thoughts and views, thus leading to unwholesome behaviour. Consequently, 'a great deal of the sickness which afflicts humanity has its origin in the mind and can only be cured by restoring the mind to health. There are very many more than we imagine, who are sick mentally.' However, when wholesome activities (e.g: listening to uplifting music) and practices (e.g: mediation on Sacred text) replace the negativity, healing for the mind can occur.

White, E. G. (2000). *Mind, Character & Personality Vol. 2* (Hagerstown, MD: Review & Herald Publishing Association), p.63.

29.

Summary

- As Adverse Childhood Experiences (ACEs) increase in children's life, the greater the odds of them being impacted negatively by emotional physiological, psychological and social issues.

- Adverse Childhood Experiences (ACEs) such as child abuse and neglect lead to trauma in children's life.

- Various ACEs negatively affect parts of the brain such as the prefrontal cortex and the limbic system.

- Interventions such as music therapy, spirituality and low-carbohydrate, high-fibre diet can repair damaged PFC or limbic system.

a) Remember to take some time to go through the Section entitled 'Intellectual Wellness' on **pages 21-22** in *Set the Captives Free (Resource Guide)*.

b) Turn to Chapter 12 and engage in the week's reading –'A Touch of Care' in *Raising the Wounded: Grasping for Hope in the Midst of Despair*.

Insightful Perspectives

Lifestyle Matters

1. Review the Activities

Review all the activities you have been asked to engage in during the last twelve (12) weeks. Are you applying the concepts in your life? In order to gauge your progress, evaluate yourself using the sub-headings below, by circling the appropriate letter (A, B or C). *The superscript numbers following each item indicate the session where each lifestyle matter is found.*

A   I have **consistently changed/ added/ been involved** in these activities.

B   I have **partially changed/ added / been involved** in the following activities on a weekly basis

C   At this stage, I still have not **changed/ added/ been involved** in these activities in my schedule.

Lifestyle Tasks	Scale		
Flush the mind through wholesome activities[1, 10]	A	B	C
Consistent physical Exercise Activities[1,2, 8, 9]	A	B	C
Learn about and practice self-awareness[1, 2]	A	B	C
Adequate water intake[2, 6, 8, 9]	A	B	C
Engage in spiritual disciplines (Devotions)[1,2,3]	A	B	C
Identify your degree of emotional wounded-ness[3]	A	B	C
Identify your emotional type/style of relating[1]	A	B	C
Engage in spiritual disciplines (Intercessory Prayer)[1,2,3]	A	B	C
Replace negative thoughts with inspired material[2, 6, 8]	A	B	C
Practise spiritual activities (Reading sacred material)[3]	A	B	C
Implement goals for self-care and wellness [2, 3, 5, 6, 10]	A	B	C
Engage in diet and sleep detox[3, 10]	A	B	C
Practise Goal-setting[3, 6, 7, 11]	A	B	C
Engage in spirituality (Theological Reflection)[4, 5]	A	B	C
Select moody foods[4, 10]	A	B	C
Monitor emotional eating[4]	A	B	C
Practise spirituality (meditation/reflection)[4,5,6,7,10]	A	B	C
Building relationships[5, 6, 8, 9, 10]	A	B	C
Learning to reframe difficult emotional issues[5]	A	B	C
Reprogramme the brain[5]	A	B	C
Building spiritual esteem[7]	A	B	C
Paving the path for emotional freedom[7]	A	B	C
Building resilience[8]	A	B	C
Creating a genogram[9, 10, 11]	A	B	C
Massage therapy[10]	A	B	C
Music intervention[11]	A	B	C

2. Plans & Goal Setting

The activities for which you have marked with **A, well done!** On the lines below, write out **a plan for each Lifestyle activity** you need to adopt /start to practise from the list above. State the possible time of the day or of the week (e.g morning, afternoon; weekends) that you will seek to incorporate your new habits.

....

....

....

....

....

....

....

....

....

....

....

....

....

....

....

....

....

....

....

....

....

....

3. Alternatively, review the plans that you may have set out for yourself. Share how you plan to begin implementing the activities you marked **with B.**

....
....
....
....
....
....
....
....
....
....
....
....
....
....
....
....
....
....
....
....
....
....

4. Review **Page 253** above, and focus on the activities which you marked with **C.** How can you implement them?

....

....

....

....

....

....

....

....

....

....

....

....

....

....

....

....

....

....

....

....

....

....

....

          VICTOR MARSHALL

Personal Reflection (WEEK 12)

- What emotional, physical, psychological, relational, social or spiritual progress have you made DURING this programme?

....
....
....
....
....
....
....
....
....
....
....
....
....
....
....
....
....
....
....
....

- What major area do you need to address emotionally, physically, psychologically, relationally, socially or spiritually?

....

....

....

....

....

....

....

....

....

....

....

....

....

....

....

....

....

....

....

....

....

....

VICTOR MARSHALL

- Identify **three (3)** areas of your life which you desire to change. What can you do to bring about these changes?

....

....

....

....

....

....

....

....

....

....

....

....

....

....

....

....

....

....

....

....

....

....

Emotional Health Lifestyle Scorecard

Week _____

ACTIVITY	DAY OF THE WEEK AND DATE						
	Sun ----/----/----	Mon ----/----/----	Tues ----/----/----	Wed ----/----/----	Thurs ----/----/----	Fri ----/----/----	Sat ----/----/----
Spiritual Engagement * Prepare for the journey of restoration with spiritual practices (See *Set the Captives Free Workbook*, pp.15, 73							
Relationship Building Pray for a particular family member/relative/ friend with whom you are having difficulty							
Exercise Engage in Exercise. State the type and amount of time daily							
Goal-setting Identify two or three things you wish to accomplish daily AND MONTHLY. This inspires hope and optimism in that you would have accomplished a goal							
Discussion Time * Identify any two (2) issues to be addressed with a particular family member/relative/friend, and prayerfully talk to that person about the issues							
Personal Reflection How much time have you spent on the reflection activity at the end of each **SESSION?**							
Special Reading On a daily basis, read ten (10) verses from the Gospel of St Mark 1-12. Also identify and **MEMORISE** the verse that attracts you.	*Verses Read*	*Verses Read*	*Verses Read*	*Verses Read*	*Verses Read*	*Verses Read*	*Verses Read* ....
Favourite Verse(s)							
Water How many glasses of water did you drink during the day?							

NOTE: * Place a tick (√) in the box next to these items to show that you have completed the activity on a daily basis. It is expected that these activities will take time and will be on-going.

NOTES

Feel free to use this space to write out the verse you are memorising from the chapter you have read this week, as a way of helping you internalise the text.

APPENDIX

Appendix A

<u>Emotional Healthy Lifestyle Scorecard (Alternative)</u>

Emotional Health Lifestyle Scorecard

Week _____

ACTIVITY	DAY OF THE WEEK AND DATE						
	Sun	Mon	Tues	Wed	Thurs	Fri	Sat
	----/----/----	----/----/----	----/----/----	----/----/----	----/----/----	----/----/----	----/----/----
Spiritual Engagement * Prepare for the journey of restoration with spiritual practices (See *Set the Captives Free Workbook*, pp.15, 73							
Relationship Building Pray for a particular family member/relative/ friend with whom you are having difficulty							
Exercise Engage in Exercise. State the type and amount of time daily							
Goal-setting Identify two or three things you wish to accomplish daily AND MONTHLY. This inspires hope and optimism in that you would have accomplished a goal							
Discussion Time * Identify any two (2) issues to be addressed with a particular family member/relative/friend, and prayerfully talk to that person about the issues							
Personal Reflection How much time have you spent on the reflection activity at the end of each **SESSION**?							
Special Reading On a daily basis, read ten (10) verses from the Gospel of St Mark 1-12. Also identify and **MEMORISE** the verse that attracts you. .... *Favourite Verse(s)*	*Verses Read*	*Verses Read*	*Verses Read*	*Verses Read*	*Verses Read*	*Verses Read*	*Verses Read* ....
Water How many glasses of water did you drink during the day?							

NOTE: * Place a tick (√) in the box next to these items to show that you have completed the activity on a daily basis. It is expected that these activities will take time and will be on-going.

266 |

Emotional Health Lifestyle Scorecard

Week _____

ACTIVITY	Sun --/--/--	Mon --/--/--	Tues --/--/--	Wed --/--/--	Thurs --/--/--	Fri --/--/--	Sat --/--/--
Spiritual Engagement * Prepare for the journey of restoration with spiritual practices (See *Set the Captives Free Workbook*, pp.15, 73							
Relationship Building Pray for a particular family member/relative/ friend with whom you are having difficulty							
Exercise Engage in Exercise. State the type and amount of time daily							
Goal-setting Identify two or three things you wish to accomplish daily AND MONTHLY. This inspires hope and optimism in that you would have accomplished a goal							
Discussion Time * Identify any two (2) issues to be addressed with a particular family member/relative/friend, and prayerfully talk to that person about the issues							
Personal Reflection How much time have you spent on the reflection activity at the end of each **SESSION**?							
Special Reading On a daily basis, read ten (10) verses from the Gospel of St Mark 1-12. Also identify and **MEMORISE** the verse that attracts you.	*Verses Read*	*Verses Read*	*Verses Read*	*Verses Read*	*Verses Read*	*Verses Read*	*Verses Read*
Favourite Verse(s)							....
Water How many glasses of water did you drink during the day?							

NOTE: * Place a tick (√) in the box next to these items to show that you have completed the activity on a daily basis. It is expected that these activities will take time and will be on-going.

Emotional Health Lifestyle Scorecard

Week _____

ACTIVITY	DAY OF THE WEEK AND DATE						
	Sun ----/----/----	Mon ----/----/----	Tues ----/----/----	Wed ----/----/----	Thurs ----/----/----	Fri ----/----/----	Sat ----/----/----
Spiritual Engagement * Prepare for the journey of restoration with spiritual practices (See *Set the Captives Free Workbook*, pp.15, 73							
Relationship Building Pray for a particular family member/relative/friend with whom you are having difficulty							
Exercise Engage in Exercise. State the type and amount of time daily							
Goal-setting Identify two or three things you wish to accomplish daily AND MONTHLY. This inspires hope and optimism in that you would have accomplished a goal							
Discussion Time * Identify any two (2) issues to be addressed with a particular family member/relative/friend, and prayerfully talk to that person about the issues							
Personal Reflection How much time have you spent on the reflection activity at the end of each **SESSION**?							
Special Reading On a daily basis, read ten (10) verses from the Gospel of St Mark 1-12. Also identify and **MEMORISE** the verse that attracts you.	*Verses Read*	*Verses Read*	*Verses Read*	*Verses Read*	*Verses Read*	*Verses Read*	*Verses Read*
Favourite Verse(s)	....	....	....	....	....	....	....
Water How many glasses of water did you drink during the day?							

NOTE: * Place a tick (√) in the box next to these items to show that you have completed the activity on a daily basis. It is expected that these activities will take time and will be on-going.

Emotional Health Lifestyle Scorecard

Week _____

ACTIVITY	DAY OF THE WEEK AND DATE						
	Sun ----/----/----	Mon ----/----/----	Tues ----/----/----	Wed ----/----/----	Thurs ----/----/----	Fri ----/----/----	Sat ----/----/----
Spiritual Engagement * Prepare for the journey of restoration with spiritual practices (See *Set the Captives Free Workbook,* pp.15, 73							
Relationship Building Pray for a particular family member/relative/ friend with whom you are having difficulty							
Exercise Engage in Exercise. State the type and amount of time daily							
Goal-setting Identify two or three things you wish to accomplish daily AND MONTHLY. This inspires hope and optimism in that you would have accomplished a goal							
Discussion Time * Identify any two (2) issues to be addressed with a particular family member/relative/friend, and prayerfully talk to that person about the issues							
Personal Reflection How much time have you spent on the reflection activity at the end of each **SESSION?**							
Special Reading On a daily basis, read ten (10) verses from the Gospel of St Mark 1-12. Also identify and **MEMORISE** the verse that attracts you.	*Verses Read*	*Verses Read*	*Verses Read*	*Verses Read*	*Verses Read*	*Verses Read*	*Verses Read*
.... *Favourite Verse(s)*	....	....	....	....	....	....	....
Water How many glasses of water did you drink during the day?							

NOTE: * Place a tick (√) in the box next to these items to show that you have completed the activity on a daily basis. It is expected that these activities will take time and will be on-going.

Emotional Health Lifestyle Scorecard

Week _____

ACTIVITY	DAY OF THE WEEK AND DATE						
	Sun ----/----/----	Mon ----/----/----	Tues ----/----/----	Wed ----/----/----	Thurs ----/----/----	Fri ----/----/----	Sat ----/----/----
Spiritual Engagement * Prepare for the journey of restoration with spiritual practices (*See Set the Captives Free Workbook*, pp.15, 73							
Relationship Building Pray for a particular family member/relative/ friend with whom you are having difficulty							
Exercise Engage in Exercise. State the type and amount of time daily							
Goal-setting Identify two or three things you wish to accomplish daily AND MONTHLY. This inspires hope and optimism in that you would have accomplished a goal							
Discussion Time * Identify any two (2) issues to be addressed with a particular family member/relative/friend, and prayerfully talk to that person about the issues							
Personal Reflection How much time have you spent on the reflection activity at the end of each **SESSION**?							
Special Reading On a daily basis, read ten (10) verses from the Gospel of St Mark 1-12. Also identify and **MEMORISE** the verse that attracts you. .... *Favourite Verse(s)*	*Verses Read*	*Verses Read*	*Verses Read*	*Verses Read*	*Verses Read*	*Verses Read*	*Verses Read* ....
Water How many glasses of water did you drink during the day?							

NOTE: * Place a tick (√) in the box next to these items to show that you have completed the activity on a daily basis. It is expected that these activities will take time and will be on-going.

VICTOR MARSHALL

Appendix B

<u>Resource for the De-cluttering Task</u>

Page 37 (Task 1)

Reflect on an unresolved issue which you have been struggling with for a while. Use the space below to engage in expressive writing (writing therapy).

The issue which I have reflected on and am prepared to face and address is ....

....

....

....

Today, on .... 20....., I endeavour to de-clutter my mind/thoughts of this issue which has been bothering/creating difficulties for me for over.. weeks/months/years.

BEGIN TO WRITE ABOUT IT **BELOW.**

....

....

....

....

....

....

....

....

....

....

....

....

VICTOR MARSHALL

....
....
....
....
....
....
....
....
....
....
....
....
....
....
....
....
....
....
....
....
....
....
....
....

VICTOR MARSHALL

....

....

....

....

....

....

....

....

....

....

....

....

....

....

....

....

....

....

....

....

....

....

....

....

Appendix C

<u>Spiritual Resources</u>

<u>Spiritual Resources</u>

<u>Resource Sheets for Pages 15 and/or 73 in *Set the Captives Free Workbook*</u>

*Use the space below to write your ideas, responses and thoughts for the activities on **Pages 15 and/ or 73** in the workbook*

....

....

....

....

....

....

....

....

....

....

....

....

....

....

....

....

....

....

....

VICTOR MARSHALL

VICTOR MARSHALL

....
....
....
....
....
....
....
....
....
....
....
....
....
....
....
....
....
....
....
....
....
....
....
....

....
....
....
....
....
....
....
....
....
....
....
....
....
....
....
....
....
....
....
....
....
....
....
....
....

VICTOR MARSHALL

Appendix D

<u>Self-awareness Perspectives</u>

MY FRIEND'S/SPOUSE'S/SIBLING'S/ RELATIVE'S VIEW OF ME AS A PERSON

The individual who has given you this form needs your honest opinion of him/her. Please complete the following by responding to the questions as honest as you can.

a) Identify two (2) values your friend/spouse/sibling/relative holds dearly? Eg. Honesty

_____

_____

_____

_____

b) What is his/her major philosophy in life?

_____

_____

_____

_____

c) How does he/she normally react when someone close to him/her tells him off /her off OR criticises him/her?

_____

_____

_____

_____

d) How does he/she normally react when someone at his/her workplace/ college/ church/ university/ club tells him off/her off OR criticises his/her?

_____

_____

_____

VICTOR MARSHALL

e) Share two (2) things he/she does unconsciously, but require someone to alert him/her about them. For example, **He/she does not look at a person when speaking to others; he/she speaks too quickly; he/she interrupts a person when he/she is speaking with to that person.**

_____

_____

_____

_____

f) Share ONE (1) rule which he/she lives by daily? Eg. **I will not be late.**

_____

_____

_____

g) How positive is the person's attitude towards people in general? Please rate it on the scale below.

Not Positive					Positive				Very Positive	
0	1	2	3	4	5	6	7	8	9	10

Please return the **completed form to your friend/relative/sibling/spouse** as soon as possible. Ensure you **HAVE NOT** written you name on it.

MY FRIEND'S/SPOUSE'S/SIBLING'S/
RELATIVE'S VIEW OF ME AS A PERSON

The individual who has given you this form needs your honest opinion of him/her. Please complete the following by responding to the questions as honest as you can.

a) Identify two (2) values your friend/spouse/sibling/relative holds dearly? Eg. Honesty

_____

_____

_____

_____

b) What is his/her major philosophy in life?

_____

_____

_____

_____

c) How does he/she normally react when someone close to him/her tells him off /her off OR criticises him/her?

_____

_____

_____

_____

d) How does he/she normally react when someone at his/her workplace/ college/ church/ university/ club tells him off/her off OR criticises his/her?

_____

_____

_____

e) Share two (2) things he/she does unconsciously, but require someone to alert him/her about them. For example, **He/she does not look at a person when speaking to others; he/she speaks too quickly; he/she interrupts a person when he/she is speaking with to that person.**

_____

_____

_____

_____

f) Share ONE (1) rule which he/she lives by daily? Eg. **I will not be late.**

_____

_____

_____

_____

g) How positive is the person's attitude towards people in general? Please rate it on the scale below.

Not Positive					Positive					Very Positive
0	1	2	3	4	5	6	7	8	9	10

Please return the **completed form to your friend/relative/sibling/spouse** as soon as possible. Ensure you **HAVE NOT** written you name on it.

References

1   This biblical material can be found in the Old Testament book of Jeremiah 8:22 in the Amplified Bible Version.

2   Ellen G. White, *Medical Ministry* (Boise, Idaho: Pacific Press Publication Association, 1932), p. 291.

3   Reference for this perspective can be found in the New Testament book of the Gospel of John 10:10.

4   The word in Hebrew for God indicates the One who is of divine nature.

Printed in the United States
by Baker & Taylor Publisher Services